Now That's a
Idea!

Michelle & Jonathan,

For His Glory!

Shirley Kimball

Now That's a GREAT *Idea!*

Nuggets of Truth that Will Change Your World!!!

How to Live on a Shoestring and Have a Blast!

Shirley Kimball

Outskirts Press, Inc.
Denver, Colorado

The opinions expressed in this manuscript are solely the opinions of the author and do not represent the opinions or thoughts of the publisher. The author has represented and warranted full ownership and/or legal right to publish all the materials in this book.

Now That's A GREAT Idea!
Nuggets of Truth that Will Change Your World!!!
How to Live on a Shoestring and Have a Blast!
All Rights Reserved.
Copyright © 2011 Shirley Kimball
Unless otherwise indicated, Bible quotations are taken from the New American Standard version of the Bible. Copyright 1973 by Foundation Press Publications.
v2.0

Cover Photo © 2011 JupiterImages Corporation. All rights reserved - used with permission.

This book may not be reproduced, transmitted, or stored in whole or in part by any means, including graphic, electronic, or mechanical without the express written consent of the publisher except in the case of brief quotations embodied in critical articles and reviews.

Outskirts Press, Inc.
http://www.outskirtspress.com

ISBN: 978-1-4327-5063-3

Outskirts Press and the "OP" logo are trademarks belonging to Outskirts Press, Inc.

PRINTED IN THE UNITED STATES OF AMERICA

Dedication

That's A GREAT Idea! I can't tell you how many times people said that to me. One day it occurred to me that if in fact these truly were "Great Ideas" that I should not keep them to myself or take them to the grave with me, but rather, I should write a book! I tend to run creative, am left handed, sometime ambidextrous (especially when playing tennis, bowling or ironing ... which I don't do much of any more!), and generally a "think outside the box" kind of person. I'm an optimist, have grown up confident, loyal and definitely have a zest for life and an unspeakable joy! So join me on this adventure and I hope something within these pages inspires you!

Publishing a book may mean that it only sells one copy – the one I buy! Or ..., it could take off and open doors beyond my wildest dreams. The future is unforeseen, but it certainly has been fun putting it together and I sensed it was given to me by the Lord to help others. It takes years to accumulate knowledge and figure things out ... then it is time to share so others can benefit and be blessed.

A special thank you to all of my family, friends, acquaintances and the wonderful people I have met over the years that have been an inspiration and encouragement to me. Some of you will see yourself in these pages as you have colored my world! For those who have benefited from these ideas, I'm thankful I could touch your life in a meaningful way.

I Praise the Lord for our son, Josh, and I dedicate this book to him. He has brought enormous joy into my life as I have watched him grow into a very talented young man. He has inspired me in so many ways, time and again. My prayer is that somehow I may always be the wind beneath his wings as he soars to new heights, completes his college years and blossoms into his medical career. He truly is a joy to know. I love you, son, and am so very thankful for you!

Table of Contents

Topics to inspire you and move you to action so you can enjoy the blessings!

Whether you are looking for "Nuggets of Truth That Will Change Your World" or desire to learn "How to Live on a Shoestring (be frugal) and Have a Blast" you're in for an adventure … It's time to "think outside the box!"

Chapter 1 .... Page 1

- **Clothes Galore & More** – Thrift Shops are everywhere and you'd be amazed what people give away … some items still have new tags on them!

  - *Are you ready for that cruise or special dinner dance!*
  - *How about a dinner date?*
  - *To the beach, a cruise to an island … or was it a ski trip you wanted?*
  - *Laugh all the way home!*
  - *Spend a few dollars on accessories – Earrings, necklaces, scarves, belts, shoes – to dress up most any outfit and bring out your personality!*

Chapter 2 .... Page 7

✓ <u>So you want to loose 10 lbs ... What "Rings Your Bell?"</u>

- *Choose Wisely – It's YOU and YOUR Future that You Are Investing In!*
- *Breakfast – The most important meal of Your day!*
- *Snacks – 10:30 AM and 4:00 PM*
- *Salads – Delicious Toppings make all the difference*
- *Trampolines, Dancing, Biking, Aerobics and Exercise*
- *Double Time! Exercise while at your desk at work!*
- *Get out your blender and use it!*

Chapter 3 .... Page 17

✓ <u>Travel with the best of them -Learn the Secrets and Never Pay Full Price!</u>

- *Realize Now the Question is NOT <u>"How can I ever afford to Travel?"</u> ... but rather <u>"Where do I want to go?"</u>*
- *Frequent Flyer Miles are a wonderful gift ... so where are yours?*
- *Be wise and learn how to Double Dip!*
- *Things to know about Frequent Flyer Miles / FF Points / Reward Programs*
- *Questionnaire Form - What Should I Ask Credit Card Companies?*
- *So where was it you wanted to travel to?*

Chapter 4 .... Page 29

✓ <u>Eating Royally While You Travel – Some of Your Favorite Foods</u>

- *Pack your cooler before leaving home and enjoy*

- *Take a candle and eat by candlelight on your balcony overlooking the ocean*
- *Electric skillet or Electric Rice Cooker*
- *Tropical Birthday Celebrations*

Chapter 5 .... Page 35

- ✓ **Attitude / Attraction / Acceptance**

  - *Are you a thermometer or a thermostat?*
  - *Life is 10% what happens to you and 90% how you respond to the circumstances*
  - *Attitude = 100%*
  - *Attitude is More Important than Aptitude!*
  - *The Vine … as part of the branch and attached to the tree!*
  - *Food for Thought!*
  - *The Weaver*

Chapter 6 .... Page 47

- ✓ **Starting A Job Search … Finding A Job … "Houston, We've Got A Problem!"**

- ✓ *Things to Remember When Starting a Job Search:*

- ✓ *Being Prepared for Your Job Interview*

- ✓ *Job Interview Questionnaire … See Appendix*

Chapter 7 .... Page 59

✓ <u>Success …</u>

- *What is your definition of success?*
- *Love Languages … Success in communicating with those you love*
- *Intentionally Desire to Serve One Another …*
- *How To Forgive (WOW!) …*
- *Keys to Healthy Communication*
- *Four Rules for Good Communication*

Chapter 8 .... Page 69

✓ <u>Counseling – Uncle Earl … Truths that Transform</u>

- *The Sandwich approach*
- *Calendar and Stars*
- *List of Family Rules with Consequences – No Yelling Zone*
- *The "I Lost It Box" … $ … A Verse to Memorize*
- *Other Resources*

Chapter 9 .... Page 75

✓ <u>Life Lessons …</u>

- *Pink & Blue Sunglasses*
- *Love Languages – Do You Know Yours?*
- *God's Word*
- *Seven Tips for Prayerful Parents*

- *Take Authority*
- *Website Resources*
- *What Blood Type Are You?*
- *Giving the Gift of Life*
- *Give of Your Time and Talents*
- *Wish List / Expenses / Savings / Giving*
- *Gain Interest and Grow Your Investment Without Loosing Your Principal! Learn about CD's and Annuities.*
- *Parents, Have You Reviewed Your Will Lately?*
- *Choose Your Battles*
- *Teach Another to Fish*
- *Shoes*
- *Questions to Ask Before You Marry!*
- *Where Are You Looking?*

Chapter 10..Page 105

✓ **Lots of "General Tips" you may find helpful!**

- *A potpourri of topics to tickle your funny bone and help you "think outside the box!"*

Chapter 11..Page 137

✓ **Quotable Quotes ...**

- *Some serious, some to make you smile, and some to make you laugh!*

Chapter 12..*Page 143*

✓ <u>**Food for Thought …**</u>

- *Recipes for You*
- *A Recipe for Each New Day*

Chapter 13..*Page 153*

✓ <u>**Just for Fun, Encouragement, Things to Brighten Your Day, Every Day!**</u>

In this chapter I have included a variety of websites for you to visit to brighten your day! Some are funny, some are delightful, some are thought provoking, some heart touching, and some will lift your spirits and make you smile.

Chapter 14..*Page 157*

✓ <u>**Suggestions for Overall Health**</u>

- *Plant New Seeds Today!*
- *Overcoming Panic Attacks*
- <u>*Healing ADD & ADHD*</u>
- *Building Lasting Relationships – Johnnie Parker*
- <u>*The Purpose Driven Woman*</u> *… Observe how she lived and learn from her actions*
- <u>*Homeopathic Doctors … Viva La Difference!*</u>
- <u>*Medical studies on the Mangosteen Fruit … Possibly Just What Your Body Needs!*</u>
  - ❖ <u>*The "Queen of Fruits" … Mangosteen*</u>

Chapter 15..Page 173

- ✓ **Excellent Books to Read, DVD & Video Series, and Some of My Favorite Songs**

- ✓ Attitude, Perspective, Success

- ✓ Communication

- ✓ Life Issues

- ✓ Medical

- ✓ Some of My Favorite Songs: Open your web-browser and enjoy viewing and listening to these on *www.youtube.com*

Appendix … **Lots of Helpful Questionnaires and Other Items for You!**....Page 193

- ✓ *Questions to Ask During Phone Interview for Job*

- ✓ *Job Pointers … Things to Remember*

- ✓ *Job Interview Questionnaire*

- ✓ *Renting A Room*

- ✓ *Questions to Ask "Before You Marry!"*

- ✓ *Medical Questionnaire Sample to Use When You are Choosing Your Insurance*

- ✓ *CD's and Annuities*

Reflections ....*Page 235*

When it's all said and done, you won't see a U-Haul behind your hearse in your funeral procession!

Don't save it all for Christmas!!!

Live Well, Laugh Often, Love One Another!

About the Author .... *Page 239*

Chapter 1

✓ **<u>Clothes Galore & More</u>** – Thrift Shops are everywhere and you'd be amazed what people give away … some items still have new tags on them!

> - *Are you ready for that cruise or special dinner dance!*

We all know that opportunity presents itself in a moment's notice, and if you're not ready, it can cost you more than you wanted to spend or would need to spend if you had prepared in advance.

You will soon learn that many people buy things in hopes of "fitting into it" someday, or just decide with the change of the seasons to clean out their closet and give beautiful things away … some still with the tags on them! So why shouldn't you enjoy what they are basically giving away? Have you ever been to a thrift shop or yard sale? If not, decide to go for the adventure and you may be pleasantly surprised at what you find. It could be a gorgeous pair of slacks, a new dress, summer capris, shorts, blouse, knit top, a brand new coffee maker or maybe a bedspread that perfectly matches your guest room.

If you are somehow not pleased with what you find in the first thrift shop, check your yellow pages and visit some others in your area. Consignment shops are always more expensive since people who drop off the items are looking for a check from the store when their items sell. Either way, there are amazing things that have been handpicked from a variety of expensive stores waiting for you to discover and enhance your wardrobe, or your household.

Some people say, "I'm sure you can find lots of things, but I'm really tiny ... or I'm bigger and they probably wouldn't have my size." Trust me, you may have to look in more than one store, but I assure you I've seen it all from the tiniest to the largest and looking is half the adventure. Finding is the joy. And, getting those items for a few dollars will make you smile too!

Now for those of you who are "germaphobics," that's why they make germicidal liquid that you just put in your washing machine along with your favorite laundry soap and they will come out just like new! Other items you can take to the $1.98 cleaners in your area and have your new items dry cleaned, pressed and ready for wearing. Another idea would be to simply wash them in Woolite.

I remember one time I was visiting my parent's beach cottage and, after spending time at the beach enjoying the waves and the summer sun, we always made it a point to stop by 4 or 5 different thrift shops in their area. My dad is a "Mr. Fix It" and always loves to look at the guy stuff, tools, books, lamps and music tapes. Mom sometimes looks at the linens and finds things for others. I enjoy the whole store and have to check out each department. It's such an adventure and you just never know what you might find!

- ***How about a dinner date?***

I am reminded of a day when I walked into a thrift shop that was not as well kept as some, and just decided to look around. Near the rear of the store was a gorgeous dress on a mannequin that was suited for a dinner dance. I was in a hurry and didn't have time to try it on. When I asked the price they said $1.00. Yes one dollar. I paid for it, took it home, and tried it on. It fit me like a glove! I got so many compliments at the Christmas dinner dance and smiled delightfully as I knew it had not cost me a small fortune!

- *To the beach, a cruise to an island ... or was it a ski trip you wanted?*

When you take a cruise, you may want something light and airy with a relaxed fit. I happened to find these cute tops with lightweight matching slacks that would be perfect for such an occasion. Another time, I was with my parents at their cottage, and we stopped in a thrift shop and found this awesome ski jacket that now hangs in my closet and I've worn many winters!

- *Laugh all the way home!*

Make it a treasure hunt and go with an open mind. You will be surprised at what you are able to purchase very inexpensively, the ideas it gives you for redecorating a room, or a nice addition to match something already in your closet. I promise you ... you will laugh all the way home! In these tough economic times your bank account will thank you. And, laughter is a great stress reliever and very good medicine for the soul.

- *Spend a few dollars on accessories – Earrings, necklaces, scarves, belts, shoes - to dress up most any outfit and bring out your personality!*

Now that you have a growing wardrobe with some things that match beautifully and make you look like a million dollars, go ahead and find a few pieces of jewelry that compliment your outfits. They certainly don't have to be expensive, just something you like! Craft fairs sometimes have some lovely and unusual pieces. Kiosks at the mall also have a fun variety of jewelry. Some craft stores will even teach you how to make jewelry (and many other lovely items). Of course, there's always your local stores where you shop, but I encourage you to explore these options outside of your standard department store. Jewelry adds a nice final touch, along with the right shoes to compliment your outfit!

I have found some of the nicest cushioned shoes in places like Payless Shoes, Walmart, Target, etc. Payless also has great metatarsal cushions that fit in most shoes and give you that extra cushion we ladies all appreciate when wearing heals! Oh, and don't forget to pick up a few fun scrunchies at your local dollar store or anywhere you shop. Most gals use them to pull up their long hair. Some of us that have short hair use them as a "pocket scarf" in a ladies suit! Just pin them in from the underside so they don't work their way up and out of your pocket! They are fun, look great and you'll get lots of compliments!

Chapter 2

✓ <u>**So you want to loose 10 lbs ... What "Rings Your Bell?"**</u>

- *Choose Wisely – It's YOU and YOUR Future that You Are Investing In!*

Sometimes it is good to sit down and actually assess what your days and weeks look like. What I mean is, how do YOU spend the hours of your day. Do you sit at an office most of the day … or … are you running around chasing children or a soccer ball for many hours?

Truth is … We have all really known for years that if we put more food into our bodies than the calories we will actually burn in a day, it is going to turn to fat.

Our bodies are fine tuned machines that for the most part are quite capable of being the shape we would like if we feed them what they were designed to digest and not clog up Your pipes and arteries! The trouble is that many of us have been duped by the commercials, good looking items on menus and what our taste buds tell our brains would be good choices. It's time to call upon your knowledge (or get some), consult your logic, and your brain in addition to your taste buds!

Some of us have believed a lie for sooooooooo long that it will take some time and some major changes in the food choices we make for the future to begin to make a dent in our shape. Just know that TODAY is the 1st Day of the Rest of YOUR Life and YOU are In Charge of making Wise Choices to Achieve the Results YOU Want! Don't be defeated by the prospect of change. It took you a long time to get the way you are, so let's get started on the New YOU! Take charge of Your Life and Your Choices. I read a sign in Dr. Jenkins' office that said:

"If you don't take care of Your health, ... it will go away!"

That statement is worth considering and it's time to take a serious look at who You have become and how You got there. This will enable You to set a new goal and be realistic about what You put into Your mouth each and every day. Have You set Your goals? If you say, "What Goals?" Hum ... then that's part of the problem! ... Without a GOAL, You're not serious about loosing weight and making it a priority. Truth is, if You don't have a target ... how do You expect to hit it! Without a target, how will You ever know when You reach Your GOAL??? Be assured, it will take initiative, motivation and persistence. If YOU really want results, get out Your calendar, plan Your strategy, get some advise from others who have lost weight or a professional, weigh Yourself at the beginning of each week. Note each day what You eat, note if You got any exercise, and Your weight at the end of the week. YOU Will See Results if You are true to Yourself and true to YOUR Plan of weight loss. Keep in mind, if You have other medical issues to address, You should certainly see Your doctor and discuss the best plan of attack.

Set your GOALS! ... Learn to Dream Again and Believe it is possible to achieve YOUR GOALS!

Do you have people in your life who can help you and be a positive influence? Kids are great at dreaming and helping You realize Your Dreams!

Find pictures of things You would like to do! Cut out the pictures and make a collage! Then, put the collage on Your wall or refrigerator. It will motive You towards YOUR

GOALS as You "Visualize your DREAM come true!" Remember, without hope and a vision, people perish along with their dreams!

- *Breakfast – The most important meal of Your day*

I'm often amazed by the number of people who don't eat breakfast, or who "grab something" to fuel their stomach or inhale whatever they can find by 10:30 in the morning. I'm sure you've heard before that Your body needs fuel (just like your car) to run efficiently. When You decide to give it what it needs, it will definitely run more efficiently with better results! Without eating breakfast, You are asking a finely turned machine (Your body) to perform, think, rationalize, process information, drive through traffic, and arrive at a destination with a positive attitude and be ready for the day! Seriously, how can You ask Your body to do this day after day and expect to be effective if You don't give it the fuel it needs to produce the energy You need? I know that some of You do it … but lets look at how it was meant to be!

❖ Take a few minutes to actually enjoy breakfast before you run out the door. You might try adding blueberries, strawberries, peaches, Craisins (cranberry raisins), walnuts, pecans, almonds, sliced banana, wheat germ or flax seed to your bowl of cereal. Your taste buds will wake up and enjoy this delightful burst of flavor! If you say, "I don't have time" to open all of those containers in the morning … know that you can buy packages of walnuts, pecans and almonds at Trader Joe's at the best price I've found (less than most grocery stores), mix them in a container with raisins or Craisins (or both), then all you have to do is pour on a few blueberries and add your wheat germ. Yum!!! I have my mom to thank for always providing a healthy breakfast for us as we were growing up, so it became a habit for a lifetime! Thanks Mom!!! ☺

❖ Gluten Free Cereals. I like cereal with crunch. If you happen to be allergic to Gluten, some of the best tasting cereals I have found that are Gluten Free come from Trader Joes. You have a choice of Tropical Forest, Cranberry Maple Nut, and Loaded Fruit & Nut! Enjoy!!!

- ❖ An occasional omelet with turkey bacon, and half a cinnamon raisin English Muffin with a touch of butter makes my mouth water. Add orange juice or a few orange slices for good measure!

- ❖ My friend, Charlotte, is up at 4:30 AM each morning to get on the road by 5:30 AM to miss the traffic in the Washington, DC area. It makes a difference between a ½ hour commute that would become at least an hour to 1 ½ hour commute in traffic. She heats water in the microwave for 3 minutes, pours it slowly into a travel coffee type container where she has placed the contents of a packet of oatmeal. She makes a travel cup of coffee and in the car she goes to "drink her oatmeal breakfast" and drink her coffee as she drives to work.

- ▪ *Snacks – 10:30 AM and 4:00 PM*

- ❖ Snacks help to keep your metabolism levels balanced, so choose them wisely to fuel your body with what it needs so that you can think, make decisions wisely and be productive. It might be peanut butter crackers, a piece of fruit, carrot sticks or celery with a little bit of dip …

- ❖ An apple and peanut butter … or a banana and peanut butter are some of my son's favorites!

- ❖ Everyone has different favorites, but I tend towards Trail Mix from Safeway grocery store or Mountain Trail Mix from Walmart with peanuts, raisins, almonds, and a few M&M's … to which I add my combination of walnuts, almonds and pecans, and sometimes I toss in Craisins. A couple of handfuls of this high protein combination charges my sparkplugs and I'm off and running again, ready for the next challenge. I used to put some of this mixture in small snack size zip lock bags, and then I just took the whole jar to the office for handy refills!

- ▪ *Salads – Delicious Toppings make all the difference*

Have you ever been to a restaurant or eatery at the mall where you can choose from a vast array of toppings for your salad? If not, expand your horizons and treat yourself and your taste buds, and … I assure you … your waist-line will thank you!

Now that I find myself as a single mom and getting older ever year, it is wise for me to realize, most of the time, I don't need to cook a 3 course meal any more. By eating lighter and choosing a smaller plate, my body is able to process smaller quantities of food and help me to keep my somewhat girlish/woman figure.

I love protein and cook a lot of chicken with garlic, sweet basil and Krazy Janes Mixed Up Salt (look for it in the grocery store with the other salt products) for seasoning and add a little Teriyaki Sauce or Honey Dijon for even more flavor. The aroma it creates in the house is delightful and my taste buds are ready for a delicious experience! I like to cook 3 or 4 pieces of chicken. Then, I can quickly make up a salad with fresh spinach, slivered carrots, green pepper for crunch, some slices of yellow or green zucchini, and cut up one piece of the chicken, fish, or turkey. Choose your salad dressing … vinaigrettes are probably better for you, or oil and vinegar … but I happen to like the creamy ones, like Ken's Honey Mustard, Sweet Vidalia Onion dressing, Honey Dijon, etc.

Fish is also very high in protein and has little or no fat. Once again I like to cook up a few pieces and use only one piece with each salad. Add some orange slices (or mandarin oranges) for variety or Craisins, and/or Honey Sesame Sticks from Trader Joes for a delightful crunch.

Craisins … Sweetened Dried Cranberries, pecans, walnuts, slivered almonds, raisins, honey almond clusters, mandarin or tangelo orange slices, Honey Sesame Sticks (from Trader Joe's), sunflower seeds, apple slices, pine nuts, or possibly cherry tomatoes will give your taste buds a burst of flavor and you'll stick your fork back into your delicious salad for another scrumptious mouthful!

Beware that breads, though delightful and I love them too, turn to sugar and fat. In an effort to cut carbs eliminate or go very light on breads, bagels, pasta, potatoes, and cheese.

And for those of you who are soda-haulics, even the diet ones are not good for you! Read the label. If Coke can clean the corrosion from your car battery terminals, should you drink it? Do the research and learn. Continuing scientific studies have proven the health benefits of Green Tea polyphenols. Compared to Vitamin E, the anti-oxidant properties of polyphenols are up to 40 times stronger. HerbaGreen Tea taken daily provides free radical fighting components that help maintain a strong immune system. Drink this great-tasting caffeine-free herbal concentrate daily to detoxify your body and maintain good health. It comes in various flavors, is easy to carry to the office, when you travel or enjoy at home.

Learn about the benefits of highly concentrated products from HerbaSway to enhance your life, your taste buds, and get healthy! *www.herbasway.com* Just add a dropper-full of one of these delicious Green Tea products or other choices listed on their website to water and ENJOY! It costs less than buying soda and is sooooooo much better for you!!! Each 2 oz. bottle gives you 60 servings and tastes great! Other companies that distribute the Herbasway products offer coupons with discounts. So here's an extra bonus just for you!!! Take a look at the following link from the Herbs Pro website and get this $19.95 bottle for a discounted price of $10.83. Now That's a GREAT Idea!!! *http://www.herbspro.com/herbaswayherbalconcentrates.htm*

- *Trampolines, Dancing, Biking, Aerobics and Exercise*

My doctor told me that I needed to find a source of exercise as it is good for strengthening your muscles and wakes up your endorphins which boosts your emotional feeling of well being, and just makes you feel better than you would otherwise. We all need ways to lift our spirits that will give us a healthier view of our situation and our world.

You may be one who just loves to exercise and I applaud you! Some of you are the Gold's Gym variety, for others an aerobic tape is better suited. For some a bike ride to get out and see the sites, a brisk morning run, or a walk around the block may be just the ticket for you. I decided to take some dance lessons and found it put a smile on my face, was interactive, enjoyable, social, and a great form of exercise that met my needs. I figured that if any form of exercise could make me smile, it must not be all bad … and actually may be doing some good! Besides, being held in the arms of a handsome man who knows how to dance, as we glide across the floor and swirl to the music, makes me feel like "Queen for A Day!" … or at least "Queen for the Moment!" Can you hear the music now, and are your feet beginning to tap to the rhythm? Don't miss out on this opportunity as learning to fox trot, cha-cha, swing, rumba, tango and waltz is a language all its own!

I have a friend who cut her calorie intake, went dancing seven times a week and lost 31 pounds having fun! It's also a great way to meet new people as it is very "interactive" exercise that will make you smile!

- *Double Time! Exercise while at your desk at work!*

Though you may be limited in what you think you can do, here are a few suggestions:

❖ While sitting at your desk and pondering a solution, do a few circular shoulder rolls

❖ Tilt your head "s l o w l y" from side-to-side, back-to-center, and then front-to-center, then circle slowly … stretching in each direction and holding for 3 seconds. This will also help to relieve stress and tension.

❖ Sit up tall and pull in on your stomach muscles, breath in and hold it for 7 seconds. Exhale and relax your stomach muscles. Repeat 5 times.

❖ Sit up tall and tighten your buttocks muscles, breath in and hold it for 7 seconds. Exhale and relax. Repeat 5 times.

❖ Tighten both stomach and buttocks muscles and proceed as above.

❖ Sit up tall, twist at the waist as far left as you can and hold for 7 seconds. Release, come back to center. Then repeat to your right and hold.

- ❖ Cleansing Breaths – Sit up tall, breath in and hold for 5 seconds. Release slowly. Repeat 3 or more times.

   - ***Get out your blender and use it!***

- ❖ Carrots, Apples, Spinach and Light CranRaspberry Juice – This combination makes a delightful tasting beverage that is thick, filling, satisfying, easy for your stomach to digest, cleansing and will help you in your desire to eat lighter, healthier and loose weight. On occasion I use this recipe 3 times per week for dinner. Also eating half a grapefruit about a ½ hour or so before making your blender beverage will help your stomach juices get started on helping you loose weight.

- ❖ Be creative or pick up a book at the grocery store, health food store, the library, or go on-line and look up Juicing Recipes – and then use your blender so you get the benefit of the fiber, vitamins & minerals and the juice combined!

- ❖ Remember … Choose Wisely – It's YOU and Your Future that You Are Investing In!

This is a note I sent to someone who asked how I stay trim and positive …

Paula,

Thank you for all your compliments. I continue to work at making right choices in the food that I eat … fresh vegetables, fruits, cereal, chicken and fish … smaller portions to help keep my weight down, riding my bike and dancing for exercise, etc. I listen to Christian music as I find other music leads my mind astray, and I hardly ever watch TV. Every morning when I wake up and shower, I put on a little make-up to brighten my face and a touch of lipstick adds a nice touch and does wonders to light up my face. It just makes me feel better to bring out the best with a little color! Spending time in God's word and in prayer gives me strength for the day.

Life has some tough bumps in the road and sometimes it is hard to find our way back. God has given each of us various gifts and talents. It is in finding those and putting them to use that we often times find happiness, purpose and joy.

<u>Philippians 3:12-14</u> ... I press on in order that I may lay hold of that for which also I was laid hold of by Christ Jesus ... but one thing I do, forgetting what lies behind and reaching forward to what lies ahead, I press on toward the goal for the prize of the upward call of God in Christ Jesus.

Blessings,
Shirley

Chapter 3

✓ <u>**Travel with the best of them – Learn the secrets and never pay full price!**</u>

- *Realize Now the Question is NOT <u>"How can I ever afford to Travel?"</u> ... but rather <u>"Where do I want to go?"</u>*

For years I noted that the people I worked for flew for business and also accrued very large numbers of frequent flyer miles, however, they never seemed willing to offer some to me! Soooooo, I made it my goal to figure out how to obtain frequent flyer miles so I too would be able to fly for ***FREE!***

I began research and discovered that credit card companies offered ***FREE*** Frequent Flyer Miles, most offering 1 Mile for every $1.00 spent. With most, it also takes about 20,000 Frequent Flyer Miles to get a ***FREE*** airline ticket anywhere in the Continental US. You need 35,000 Frequent Flyer Miles to travel to Hawaii and 45,000 to travel to Europe. Now before you roll right out of your chair laughing or get discouraged, think with me for a minute. If you were to look at last year's checkbook and calculate what you spend in a year, would it add up to $20,000? How about $35,000 or $45,000? Many people make at least that and some make a whole lot more per year and spend it on something. The question to ask yourself is: "Am I getting 1 ***FREE***

Frequent Flyer Mile for every $ that I spend every day?" And, if not, why not? Is the light bulb beginning to come on?

<u>*Do you realize that if you learn to think differently about how you purchase the things that you already plan to purchase, you can accrue FREE Frequent Flyer Miles that will afford you a FREE Airline Ticket, a cruise, hotel stay, or possibly a cottage at the beach!!!*</u> Do I have your attention??? How about if I told you that if you do a little research you may find a credit card that offers 2 **FREE** Miles for every $ spent, and even 3 **FREE** Miles for gas and grocery purchases!

Some of the mileage requirements have changed over the years, but so has the cost of living!

Okay, let's think about one week of your life and the types of places you spend money. The gas station for your car, the grocery store, a restaurant (even McDonalds takes credit cards), clothes, entertainment, pharmacy, even the $1.00 store often times will take your credit card as payment.

Now, for those of you who have never used a credit card and are afraid that you will overspend using your little piece of plastic, I highly encourage you to learn the first rule of purchasing. NEVER, I repeat NEVER purchase anything that you cannot afford. And, when you do purchase an item using your credit card, take the time IMMEDIATELY to write it in your check book ... (as if you had written a check), the name of the store and the amount you just spent. This will give you an immediate record of what you have spent and you can see what your running balance is so that you **<u>DO NOT</u> overspend**. You can put an X or CC (which stands for Credit Card purchase) in the box for the check # (because you didn't actually write a check), but YOU WILL RECEIVE AN INVOICE at the end of the month for the things you purchased and all items will be accounted for and YOU WILL WRITE A CHECK FOR THE FULL AMOUNT of your purchases. This way "YOU OWN your Credit Card," and YOU NEVER WANT IT TO OWN YOU! This means you are being responsible, making wise choices and will *never have to pay interest* because you "Pay Off your Full Bill Every Month." If you cannot be disciplined to work this process than I highly encourage you NOT to use a credit card and forget the joy of being rewarded with *FREE* Frequent Flyer Miles. The choice is yours!

- *Frequent Flyer Miles are a wonderful gift … so where are yours?*

I have used frequent flyer miles to fly 3 of us to California for *FREE*, another time we used some to travel to The Bahamas, fly our son home from college, 2 *FREE* airline tickets to Aruba, 3 *FREE* airline tickets to Hawaii, trips over the holidays to visit relatives, etc. The joy is just knowing that "every time I buy the things I need to purchase anyway," I can start thinking about where I would like to go next. Even if it takes you a whole year or two to accrue enough *FREE* Frequent Flyer Miles to take a trip, the question is simply where do you want to travel?

- *Be wise and learn how to Double Dip!*

Think about it. You go to work, earn $$$ and they seem to evaporate like water and you are probably not even sure where some of them go because life is full of incidentals. All those times that you run errands and stop to get this or that, or coffee, or lunch, or stop at the cleaners, or pick up a prescription, or a few groceries, or the always needed gasoline you could be getting *FREE* Frequent Flier Miles. This may not seem like much, but all these items add up and so do your miles. So, the question you have to ask yourself is: If I'm going to buy these things anyway, should I just hand out cash, write a check, OR knowing that all these items add up, should I begin changing how I pay for items and begin accruing *FREE* Frequent Flyer miles. Knowing that I can start thinking about exactly where I want to travel energizes my day! You've spent your money once, and if you paid with cash or a check it is gone and you will never see it again. If you used your credit card, you are accruing miles and you will get to benefit a "2nd time around" when you fly for *FREE*. <u>I love the word "FREE.</u>" All of this brings me to the next important point, which is learning the differences when selecting a credit card.

- *Things to know about various Credit Cards, Frequent Flyer Miles, Frequent Flyer Points, and Rewards programs*

As with most things, there are some very important things to know about yourself and about the variety of credit cards that are being offered, and I assure you *"They Are Not All the Same."* So, put on your thinking cap and I will teach you what to look for so you can be successful.

Principle #1: Know Yourself and Your Habits

- As I stated previously, you must first KNOW YOURSELF and KNOW if you are disciplined enough to ONLY BUY ITEMS YOU CAN AFFORD. *It is Extremely Important from the Start to Be Honest with Yourself about this Principle.* If not, you will find yourself in a world of debt that may take you years to pay off and even if you have a trillion FREE Frequent Flyer Miles, you will be broke and unable to use them! If You CANNOT Afford It, DON'T BUY IT! So, a word to the Wise … Be Wise and Honest with Yourself. The First Question You Want to Ask Yourself Is …Are you disciplined?

Principle #2: The Next Question you want to ask yourself is Where You Want to Travel? Is it throughout the US, Hawaii, or Caribbean, Europe, etc.

- Some Credit Cards are best used for US travel and others are better if you plan to travel overseas, to the islands and Europe. So, take a minute and think about where you want to travel? Have you seen the breathtaking Colorado Rocky Mountains, New England, Florida, Niagara Falls, the Grand Canyon, and the Painted Dessert, or the California coast? Or are the islands calling you … Hawaii, Aruba, The Caribbean, or a trip to Paris, Italy or France?

Principle # 3: Understanding the Basic Differences in Credit Cards:

- Most Credit Cards require 20,000 to 25,000 Frequent Flyer Miles for a trip anywhere in the Continental US, 35,000 nearby but outside the US, and 45,000 to Europe, etc.

- For those who just want to fly throughout the US and like to look on-line for the cheapest fare, or hot deal, you may want to consider a Credit Card where you search and find the flight you want at the best price on the Internet. Capital One works this way. You then take the price you found for the flight on the Internet x 80 to determine the number of Frequent Flyer Miles you will need. Example: If you find a round trip ticket on-line for under $300 to fly where you want to go, or need to fly a student home from college, or find a special deal to a warm sunny spot, then take the cost of the Round Trip Ticket x 80. Let's say you find a flight to Florida for $200 Round Trip. $200 x the factor of 80 = 16,000 Frequent Flyer Miles you will need to take this trip … which is a whole lot less than needing to save 20,000 – 25,000 Frequent Flyer Miles as is needed on other credit cards.

❖ If you find that airfare to places you want to travel is going to be over $300, it may be better to go with a credit card that lists basic Frequent Flyer Miles. Example: If a trip to California is $465 Round Trip, $465 x 80 − 37,200 Frequent Flyer Miles. So the better choice is to have a credit card that only charges 20,000 – 25,000 Frequent Flyer Miles to travel ANYWHERE in the US regardless of the cost of the airline ticket.

❖ Now for those of you who like to "think outside the box" track with me on this! Capital One offers a credit card where you can accrue **Double or Triple FREE Frequent Flyer Miles** for every purchase you make! You may have to pay an annual $35 fee to have these credit cards, but then again you are earning your miles much faster … and of course the factor to determine the number of miles you need to fly is slightly higher … but I have found it is well worth it and spending $35 is nothing compared to the cost of a **FREE** airline ticket! What if you could combine your **FREE** Frequent Flyer Miles on these cards that offer double and triple miles when you are ready to purchase your **FREE** ticket??? One card offers Double Miles for everything I purchase. Another card offers Triple Miles for all gasoline and grocery purchases, and One Mile for all other purchases … so I have to remember which card I use where, but the benefit is well worth it!!! Another very important factor to know is that each grocery store and gas station has a store code. This code lets Capital One know to give you Triple Miles for these purchases. *Many Target and Walmart stores are becoming super stores that also carry vegetables and fruits among other groceries. These stores have been given a "grocery store code" … which* *means no matter what you buy there, whether it is a TV, socks, or groceries, you accrue Triple Miles for all your purchases at these stores!!!* If you have questions, call Capital One to confirm the code for a store in your area.

❖ Also, know that often your Frequent Flyer Miles are good for use for any type of travel related expense, i.e. vacation rentals, airplane, train, cruises, bed & breakfasts, hotel, condo, excursions & tours. Some even include rental car ramifications, legal aid, concierge servicing, vacation set-up. Learn to call your credit card company's reward division for better benefits, amenities, restaurants, and even sporting events.

<u>**Other VERY IMPORTANT Criteria to Know**</u> when choosing a Credit Card. It's wise to check out the answers to these items before choosing your credit card.

✓ <u>**Black Out Dates – Holidays**</u> – Some Frequent Flyer Programs restrict your travel so that you cannot fly on holidays. I would not recommend a credit card with black-out restrictions.

✓ <u>**Does the credit card have an Annual Fee**</u> or No Fee for having the credit card? Why not get a credit card that does not charge you an annual fee? Why pay for something that other credit card companies give you for FREE – No Annual Fee! However, on some occasions there may be a reason to be willing to pay for a credit card, i.e. I found one that offered DOUBLE MILES and another that offered TRIPLE MILES! For every dollar I spend, I receive 2 or 3 Free Frequent Flyer Miles and these cards costs me $35 a year. For my needs, it was worth paying $35 a year to get the extra miles faster than I could accrue them with any other credit card.

✓ <u>**Do your Frequent Flyer Miles Expire after so many years**</u> (usually either 4-5 years) or are they good for many years to come with No Expiration Date? Check to see what they are offering.

✓ <u>**Can you fly on any airline**</u> ... or only one or two airlines? If you get a United

Airlines or American Airlines or any Airline Credit Card, be advised that you can only fly on that airline and their affiliates. So, let's say you see a great airfare on Southwest, Jet Blue or Continental or another airline and you don't have "their airline credit card." Sorry. Know that usually it is wiser to choose a bank credit card so you can "Fly On ANY Airline!"

- Knowing that this is a lot of information to try to absorb if you haven't thought about this process before, I have created a Questionnaire Form and included it in the Appendix to make it easy for you to think through ***How To Choose A Credit Card that's Best for YOU!*** As you know yourself better than anyone else, please take a moment to think through these questions and you'll be glad you did!

- *Questionnaire - What Should I Ask Credit Card Companies? Do Your Own Research so you get the Credit Card that is Best for You. Actual Form to Help You Decide How To Choose A Credit Card that's Best for YOU is in the Appendix*

Having a Questionnaire Form in front of you is helpful when you are researching various credit card companies, and knowing the right questions to ask is even better! You may want to make several copies of this form so you can jot down the answers to the questions as you do your research. Then you can look at your results to determine which company offers you the features you really want in a credit card that offers you ***FREE*** Frequent Flyer Miles. Every credit card company is very different and it is the wise person who will do a little research up front in order to know that you have made the best choice.

I recommend using a search engine like Yahoo or Google and putting in the words FREE Frequent Flyer Miles. View the various sites that come up and take notes on them so you can make the best choice for you!

Once you decide on the credit card that best suites your needs, consider calling your cell phone provider, your electric company, your mortgage company, your student loan company, etc. to see if they take credit card for payment of your bill without charging a fee. If so, why not get all those miles each and every month! Do you see your **FREE** Frequent Flyer Miles accumulating right before your very eyes! So, now, where was it you wanted to travel to next???

Principle #4 -- Have you learned how to use PriceLine and Bidding for Travel ???

I like to use these websites for Hotel & Rental Car Reservations because I don't really care what very nice hotel I stay at in a particular city, nor do I care which rental car company rents me a nice car. But I do care how much I am willing to pay for my hotel stay and rental car. It's all in knowing how to get the best deal and spend less for the same thing!!! It will make you smile! Thanks Eric for teaching me this very important key to enjoying discount travel prices!

- The reason these are such good tools is that every hotel and every rental car company is only making money if the rooms are full and the cars are rented. If a hotel has available rooms on the day you want to rent one, they are often willing to provide very low on-line prices to fill their rooms. Once again, an empty room on any given day brings in $0.00.

- Take a look at *www.priceline.com* and choose hotels. Put in a city and select a date, select the star quality you desire to see how this works. Price Line will show you the on-line prices that people have rented rooms for in the city you have chosen. Here's one time when last minute shopping for a hotel can be to your advantage!

- With Rental Cars, you put in the city or airport where you want to pick up your rental vehicle and the type of vehicle you desire. It will list across the board all the available rental car companies in that area and all you have to do is choose the one that is offering the best price. Paying $15 per day is a whole lot better than paying $50 per day!

- Now you have done your research and you are ready to go to *www.biddingfortravel.com* and place your bid (what you are willing to pay) for your hotel room or rental car. The system will allow you three tries with the same criteria per day. If you don't accept any of their offers, you can change the number of stars on your hotel or the type of vehicle or the dates and try again. Usually you can offer a bid that will be accepted by the third try and you can smile for all the $$$$$ you have just saved for your trip!!! If not, use what you have learned and try bidding again tomorrow!

❖ If you happen to have coupons for rental car company discounts or promotion codes, you can usually secure an even better price! Often you can find coupons at Costco, sometimes they come in the mail or in with your credit card statement, or even through AAA, AARP, or Amway Membership.

- *So where was it you wanted to travel to?*

26 • NOW THAT'S A GREAT IDEA!

CHAPTER 3 • 27

28 • NOW THAT'S A GREAT IDEA!

Chapter 4

✓ ***Eating Royally while you Travel and Enjoying Some of Your Favorite Foods***

- *Pack your cooler before leaving home and enjoy*

I am reminded of a time when I had 100,000 FREE Frequent Flyer Miles to use or loose … so, of course, I decided to use them. After being married for 21 years, being thrown into a divorce which I did not want and was not Biblical, I went into a deep depression for 5 years. After visiting many counselors, struggling to work through and comprehend my current situation, internally the switch began to turn on in my mind to decide to live again. I began to "wake up and begin to emotionally feel again." Anyone who has gone through a divorce they did not want, or another tragic loss in their life, will understand what I mean. I discovered that I had lots of Frequent Flyer Miles that had accrued during a time when I really didn't want to travel anywhere.

Even when you are depressed, you still have to buy groceries, gasoline, pay your cell phone bill and other bills (some people even pay their mortgage and college tuitions on their credit card … now that's a great way to rack up looooooooots of **FREE**

Frequent Flyer Miles)!!! Now it was time to wake up and decide to live or loose all the miles I had accrued.

My wonderful son, Josh, was busy with school and soccer, and so focused on his goals that he didn't want to travel. I had previously been to Hawaii and The Bahamas, and wanted to go somewhere I had never been. I put together an e-mail and sent it to about 15 friends asking who could take the time off (9 days) and would like to join me for a trip to Aruba, with **FREE** airfare!!! Some who really wanted to go could not get away during the time slot that worked best for me. Some had already taken their vacation time, however, two ladies were available and we began to make our plans. I had enough **FREE** Frequent Flyer Miles to fly myself and one other person at 45,000 FREE Frequent Flyer Miles needed per person. Gennene's husband had lots of Frequent Flyer Miles from business travel, so we were set.

Since Betty and I were single moms (after over 20 years of marriage), we were still looking to be as frugal as we could in making our plans, but also to have a wonderful time away from it all! Since we were all "moms," making a few meals for ourselves was easy. So, we decided our criteria for the trip was as follows. The place where we stayed had to be "On the Water, Have a Balcony Overlooking the Ocean, and Have a Kitchen/Kitchenette." Thanks to PriceLine.com and Bidding For Travel we got all three and found a delightful place to stay on the water, with a balcony and kitchenette at a greatly discounted rate! We stayed at the Amsterdam Manor Beach Resort in the tower, which had a charm all its own! *http://amsterdammanor.com/index.html* It had a great ocean view from the balcony where we sat and ate our banana walnut pancakes that we made in our kitchenette!

We had learned in talking with others that buying restaurant food on an island is expensive because it all has to be shipped in and the price goes up. So…… I called the airline we were flying and asked if it was okay to take a cooler on wheels full of food along on our trip. They approved! However, whatever food we did not use, we could not bring back to the US. So we planned our meals accordingly, decided what we all liked to eat and purchased steak, shrimp, seafood, and some items for breakfast and lunch. Each passenger was allowed two pieces of luggage, so I took a big suitcase for clothing and a cooler on wheels that we duck taped shut just to be sure it made it all in one piece just as we had packed it. Ah, yes, those whole-wheat blueberry pancakes we ate that morning out on the balcony as we watched the waves lap on the shoreline were delightful, along with the steak and shrimp dinner, etc.

- *Take a candle and eat by candlelight on your balcony overlooking the ocean*

As we were three women traveling together, romance was not what we were looking for as we ate together, but ambiance and a delightful setting makes a woman feel special. So bringing along 3 placemats and a candle gave a nice touch to an elegantly prepared delicious dinner that we made ourselves. Taking along a few spices to season our food gave us everything we needed to bring out the flavors.

- *Electric skillet or Electric Rice Cooker*

I am also reminded of a time when I was married that I actually packed an electric skillet and a rice cooker in a small rolling suitcase along with my clothing for cushioning! We didn't have much money, but we had big dreams and it was a way that we could afford to eat nice healthy meals, and only eat out a few times during the 10 days we were in Bermuda. We stayed in a lovely bed and breakfast home near the south shore that had a charm all its own. The weather was beautiful, so we just made sure the window was open to let the steam out! We bought our meats and vegetables daily at a local store and when our dinner was ready, we either ate in our room or put our food in containers with lids, road our motorbike to the beach, spread out our blanket and enjoyed dinner on the beach! A little creativity goes a long way for making a memorable moment!

- *Tropical Birthday Celebrations*

Ah, yes! This definitely puts a smile on my face as I remember the fun we had while in Aruba. We are moms and we have made many a birthday cake for our families over the years and it was now time to celebrate us! We decided before we left that we should each purchase a fun gift for each other from the dollar store. Nothing expensive, just a little something which would make us smile. It's more about just knowing someone thought of you and not about the cost of the gift! I packed one "Happy Birthday" tote bag (to reuse for the gifts), tissue paper and 3 funny birthday cards.

When we arrived on the island and learned of various activities and events, we then decided where we each wanted to go for our "Tropical Birthday Dinner Celebrations!" One chose a dinner cruise and dancing to island music on the boat. I chose to dine at Madame Jeanette's, a restaurant we were told we just had to visit with an outdoor venue, a white stone floor, beautiful lattice work with vines and a serenading vocalist who played guitar. The food was delicious and the presentation was amazing. I recommend that you visit just for the ambiance – rattan tables and comfortable chairs situated among beautifully lighted trees and torches. The experience was delightful. It was truly a great choice! Another chose to dine at an outdoor event hosted by our hotel, as we listened to the waves and watched the evening entertainment while we dined. We told the waiter whose tropical "birthday" it was that evening and played along. When it was time for dessert, some of the staff gathered around our table to sing to the "birthday girl" and we presented our gifts with laughs and smiles that made for a very enjoyable evening.

For any birthday, it is fun to make the honored guest feel special! Here are some fun, non-threatening questions to draw attention to ... and get to know the one celebrating their birthday:

❖ What was your favorite childhood activity or toy?

❖ As you think back to your childhood can you remember a very special birthday or Christmas and why?

❖ If you could travel anywhere you wanted to go unrestrained by time and money, where would you go and why?

❖ If you could drive whatever type of car you would like, what would you choose, what color would it be and why?

❖ If you could dream of something you would like to accomplish, knowing you could not fail, what would it be?

❖ What's on your bucket list? What are the things you would like to do or places you want to go to before you kick the bucket?

Another fun trip took us to Waikiki, Hawaii! Josh was a pre-med student at Campbell University in North Carolina where he completed his coursework in 3 ½ years, played college soccer all 4 years and was President of Fellowship of Christian Athletes for 3 years. I'm not sure how anybody actually does that, but he did, and he graduated Magna Cum Laude with a Bachelor of Science Degree.

While we are on the topic of "Birthdays" ... ***Never be disappointed again that "Someone Doesn't Remember Your Birthday!"*** You obviously know when it is ... so begin to speak about it! Get over the fact that it may not be on everyone else's mental radar screen. Begin to drop a few hints. About two or three weeks before "Your Birthday," you might say ... "Hum, I've been trying to decide what might be fun to do for my birthday this year." Later you might say ... "You know, I've been thinking I'd like to do this, that or the other. What do you think would be most fun?" Get some interaction going ... ***and Never be Disappointed Again!***

We had much to celebrate, and I had been saving FREE Frequent Flyer Miles for a while to make this become a reality. I asked Josh who he would like to take along on this great adventure, and he chose his college buddy, Caleb. I had never traveled with Joshua and Caleb before, but it sounded kind of Biblical and we were definitely headed for "the promised land" of Hawaii! I invited my Mom to join in the fun and as a foursome we had an awesome vacation ... and flew there for FREE. Ah, what bliss!

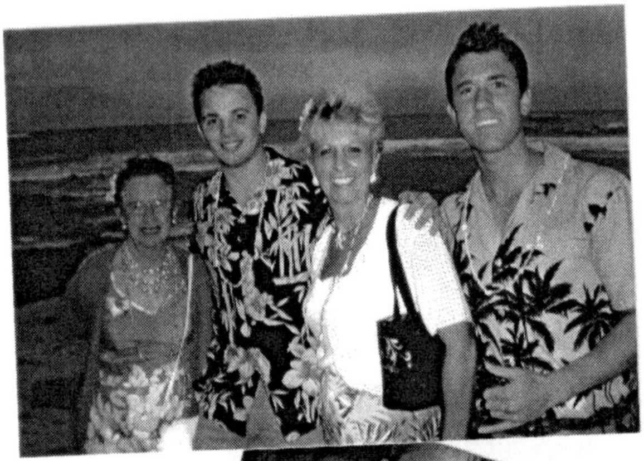

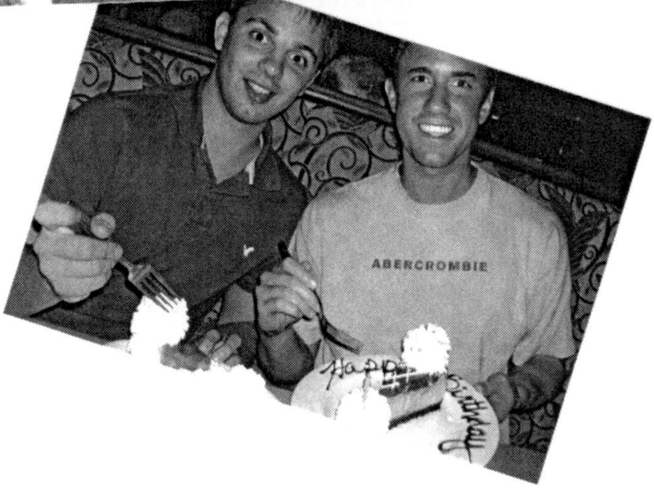
ABERCROMBIE

Chapter 5

✓ *Attitude / Attraction / Acceptance*

- *Are you a thermometer or a thermostat? A thermometer gives us the temperature of a situation --- A thermostat adjusts the surroundings!*

When you walk into a room, does it become rigid or do people smile along with you. Life is a choice and how you present yourself will determine how others respond to you. I enjoy getting in an elevator with total strangers and greeting people with a smile, and the world smiles with you (most of the time) and I haven't even said a word.

"Our lives are not determined by what happens to us, but by how we react to what happens; not by what life brings to us, but by the attitude we bring to life. A positive attitude causes a chain reaction of positive thoughts, events, and outcomes. It is a catalyst, a spark that creates extraordinary results." – Anonymous

"Sometimes our fear of doing something causes us to miss out on a new adventure. Some fear not that their life will have an end … but that it will not have a beginning!" Ron Newcomb

Don't sell yourself short. You are loved by God the Father even if your real father was not there for you. In God's eyes you are His child and he wants to get to know you and for you to get to know Him.

From one pumpkin to another!!!!!!

A woman was asked by a coworker, "What is it like to be a Christian?"

The coworker replied, "It is like being a pumpkin."

God picks you from the patch, brings you in, and washes all the dirt off of you. Then He cuts off the top and scoops out all the yucky stuff.

He removes the seeds of doubt, hate, and greed.

Then He carves you a new smiling face and puts His light inside of you to shine for all the world to see."

- ***Life is 10% what happens to you and 90% how you respond to the circumstances.***

There are definitely some things in life that do not leave room for many smiles, and I have certainly experienced some of them. As the waters calm and life rebalances, it is healthy to find the things that make you smile. It could be a walk in the park, a visit to the beach, and mountain hike, a cup of coffee with a friend, dancing, smelling a rose, reading a good book, playing with a puppy. Sometimes we just need a friend to talk to and someone to put an arm around our shoulder and understand. There is a little book titled <u>Who Moved My Cheese</u> which I found very helpful at a time when I couldn't see above my shoe tops!

My Dear Jan,

Today is the first day of the rest of our lives! We each have a blank canvas, a palate of colors and God encourages each of us to … Go paint our world!!! ☺

Today is a new chapter with new opportunities and new adventure! Live life with gusto; embrace the present because you will never get today again! Dream big as it will be the surge welling up in you to give you the energy to take each new step forward to the next lily pad on your way to seeing your dreams fulfilled.

When you keep looking in the rearview mirror, you are the only one who is still in jail, as the world and those who hurt us have moved on. Give yourself the permission to live again. Gain strength from God's Word and His promises as you are His child and you are LOVED. Smile from the inside and inform your face that you are happy, and the world will notice.

Love, blessings and hugs to you my friend,

Shirley

Jan,

Know that we love you and want to see you grow beyond this experience. Simply said, we care about you enough to walk with you through this chapter so that you can enter the next chapter wiser and with a whole heart. We've all been hurt somewhere along the way in life and it is truly painful because it leaves a hole in our heart. There is a time for grieving the loss of a relationship. There is a time for tears. We understand as we have been there. However, you have said yourself that this person was not the right one for you, so the sooner you can let it go, the sooner you will begin to look forward and live again. Each day is a new opportunity to be all that God created you to be. Begin to dream again and become all that God wants you to be.

What are your dreams? What are your hopes? What do you want to accomplish this coming year? Please read again what I wrote to you earlier today (attached below) and decide to live again.

Jan, know that the only way to grow through something is to face it head on and decide not to let it control you. Anytime something else, even if it is your own emotions that control you, you are enslaved and not free to enjoy each new day.

Acknowledge that you were not married to him. Therefore, he is free to date whomever he wishes, whether you would have made that same choice or not. He is accountable to God, not to any of us. When we start playing God we are in a heap of trouble. I'm not sure we can be fully aware of his motives, but maybe you were protected against a situation that would have hurt you even more.

References to him being bad and evil sadden me as I have trouble knowing how to process these words when we genuinely care about you and want only God's best for you. Don't let Satan take you down a sadistic path that only leads to sorrow and apathy. I am so sorry that you have been so deeply hurt by this relationship.

Proverbs 3:5-6 … Trust in the Lord with all your heart and lean not unto your own understanding, but in all your ways acknowledge Him and He will direct your paths.

In His Love,
Shirley

Jan,

Love you gal!

All the flowers of all our tomorrows are in the seeds we plant today! Enjoy planting new seeds, going new places, meeting new people! Stop to smell the flowers and enjoy God's handiwork all around you in the beauty of the blue sky, the white puffy clouds, the gentle breeze, and the sound of His creation.

We're all in this together and God is our pilot! Praying for His leading, guidance, direction … and the husband of His choice for you, me and all our friends who find themselves single later in life!!!

Love,
Shirley

- *Attitude = 100% ...* Here's a "lifestyle" tip ...

If you match the letters in the alphabet to the corresponding sequential numbers they represent ... where A = 1 and Z = 26, you'll always find that the word "attitude" = 100%

```
A =   1
T =  20
T =  20
I =   9
T =  20
U =  21
D =   4
E =   5
    100%
```

Therefore, always remember, that your "attitude" affects your "altitude."

❖ A young boy with an amazing attitude spoke words of wisdom: I'm not old enough to play baseball or football. I'm not eight yet. My Mom told me when you start baseball, you aren't going to be able to run that fast because you had an operation. I told Mom I wouldn't need to run that fast. When I play baseball, I'll just hit them out of the park. Then I'll be able to walk. – Edward J. McGrath, Jr. "An Exceptional View of Life," quoted in Chicken Soup for the Soul.

❖ When you feel like you've lost your way and can't find the light switch to clear away the darkness ... Remember in the dark what you knew to be true in the light! There is sunshine on the other side of the tunnel, but you must walk through the tunnel. Hopefully you have a friend you can confide in that will walk with you. If not, seek out a Christian Counseling Center, a church that teaches God's word, a Bible Study to help you understand you are not alone and that, believe it or not, others have walked this same path and can give you direction and help you get balance back in your life. You don't have to reinvent the wheel ... others have already walked the same path and desire to point you in the right direction. Reach out and learn to live again!

❖ If you are feeling depressed, remember that everything can seem to be difficult the first time you do it, whether its starting a new job, learning how to drive a stick shift car, or moving to a new city with no friends. Don't be so hard on yourself, and remember that a few days later, a week later, or even a month later, it will seem a lot easier. Practice makes perfect. Remember to ask a lot of questions along the way. Don't be afraid to learn something new and be stretched beyond your comfort zone! It's part of the process to maturity and makes your story much more interesting! When you are old and gray, what will be the chapters of your story that helped you "become" who you are today?

- *Attitude is More Important than Aptitude!*

I received this in an e-mail and wanted to share it with you…

If we respond to our difficulties positively, determined with God's help to overcome, we will. If we react negatively with a defeated attitude, we will be beaten, no matter how brilliant we are.

As Zig Ziglar says in his book, See You at the Top, "Attitude is much more important than aptitude.... Despite the overwhelming evidence which supports the importance of the right mental attitude, our entire educational system from kindergarten through graduate school virtually ignores this vital factor in our life. Ninety percent of our education is directed at acquiring facts with only 10 percent of our education aimed at our feelings—or attitudes.

"These figures are truly incredible when we realize that our thinking brain is only 10 percent as large as our feeling brain. A study by Harvard University revealed that 85 percent of the reasons for success, accomplishments, promotions, etc. were because of our attitudes and only 15 percent because of our technical expertise."

Ziglar also pointed out that William James, the father of American psychology, stated that the most important discovery of our time is that we can alter our lives by altering our attitudes.

"What do you do and how do you cope?" people have asked when things have gone wrong in my life.

- ❖ Express emotions. For one thing, I've learned not to deny my feelings, so when I'm hurting, I cry. God not only gave us laughter to express our joy, but tears to express our hurt and sorrow. Crying has a healing effect. It soothes the soul. Plus, when I'm frustrated, I share my feelings with a friend. Or if I'm angry, I share my feelings with the person I'm angry at or I write them out and throw away the piece of paper.

- ❖ Give thanks. I constantly make a point of giving thanks to God for the many good things in my life which far outnumber my few problems.

- ❖ Trust God. I have learned to trust God—not always without doubt or confusion. I don't always understand why bad things happen. However, one thing I do understand, while Satan and his forces of evil want to use my circumstances to try and destroy me, God wants to use them to strengthen me. The choice is mine.

The only times in my life when I have grown have been during difficult times. Who wants to change when everything is going well? Also, if there is any quality to my writing and other work, it has all come out of life's struggles.

While I don't believe in quick fixes or simplistic solutions to life's complex problems, I do know that God teaches us many lessons through difficult and challenging times—if we let him. In spite of outward appearances, I also believe that "in all things God works for the good of those who love [and trust] him"— even if it is eventually!

Can you accept your difficulties as opportunities to grow and ask God to show you what he wants you to learn through them? If so, your life will be greatly enriched.

- *The Vine ... as part of the branch and attached to the tree!*

❖ If you look in the Bible at the Book of John, Chapter 15 talks about the vine and the branches and how we are "grafted in" to God's kingdom, adopted if you will, when we accept Him as Lord and Savior of our lives! It's a free gift ... so partake and live the abundant life with the resource of His power in your life! It's kind of like a lamp sitting near a wall outlet. The outlet is available, usable, full of power and has all the resources necessary to be a source of life and energy, but you have to get "plugged in" to experience the fullness of His presence in your life! Plug In!!!

❖ If you are interested in knowing more, contact one of the following: Young Life, Campus Crusade, Fellowship of Christian Athletes, Intervarsity Christian Fellowship, your local church, Focus on the Family, Family Life Today, or McLean Bible Church in McLean, VA. You can use your favorite search engine to locate each of these.

❖ On the other hand, ... there are the vines that attach themselves to the trees in my yard. I was walking around my yard and enjoying its beauty when I noticed the pretty green and white vines growing up the branches of the Rose of Sharon bushes at the end of my driveway. Then I also noticed the stalks of blackberry bushes that were towering high above one of the tall Rose of Sharon bushes. At a closer look, I noticed that one side of the Rose of Sharon bush was dying and some of it was dead. I got out the clippers and began the process of ripping and cutting away the "pretty green and white vine" which was tightly wrapping itself around the Rose of Sharon and killing it.

❖ Though the vine had its own beauty at the base of the Rose of Sharon, it was strangling the life out of this tree. I was amazed how tightly entwined the vine had intricately attached itself with it's gazillion little roots and feelers!!! It took work getting them loose and I had to actually use the clippers to pry some of the vines away. What in your life looks good, is pretty and attractive, but is sapping the life right out of you? Food for thought! Prune it back or it will kill you or at least hold you back and do potential damage to your growth.

Here's an e-mail I sent to a gal who thinks I have it all together and she wanted some advice as to how to deal with life and depression:

Paula,

It was great seeing you at the Love & Respect series. Emerson is sooooo right on!!! I wish I had heard him speak about 25 years ago!!!

Thank you for sharing and helping me to understand the world as you see it.

A long time ago I learned that "the glass is either half empty or half full." By that I mean that our perspective on life will often direct our thoughts, our feet and our eating habits. If we think that we have no hope of fulfilling our dreams than that is how we will act, think, live and eat. It has been said many times, we are what we think we are ... and if we think we can't than we are right! It's kind of like the child's story of the little engine that "could." He believed he could climb the mountain and as friends encouraged him, he put forth more effort to reach his goal and ... he did! When we do things to motivate ourselves in the right direction, we begin to see progress, belief begins to show up on our face and then hope starts to well up in us that will encourage us as well as others.

*The book entitled **"Becoming"** talks about the fact that each day is a new day and we are to be constantly "becoming" all that God wants us to be. That means we have to not only read His word, but begin believing that He wants what is best for us. He first of all wants a relationship with us. He is the God of the universe who set the stars in the heavens and the planets spinning, put the mountains in place and separated the sky from the ocean. How can we ignore Him and think that we can direct our own lives?*

I certainly do not have it all together ... but I continue to work at it! We all have our flaws, failures and trials ... but much of how we function each day is motivated by our relationship with the Lord and doing the things we already know are good for us, i.e. ... doing whatever we can to improve on who we are and having a goal in mind. Living life with a purpose to not only please Him, but to see our lives as a vessel He has entrusted to us to manage.

Eating a solid dinner between 6-7:30 PM will probably help curb your appetite later in the evening. Anything we eat before bed just turns to fat and is hard to get rid of ... so you may want to address this so you can see progress and feel better about yourself. Sometimes a spoonful or two of yogurt and/or a few crackers will help satisfy an unsettled stomach late at night and is much better for you than ice cream, cake or other such items.

Self talk is something people do all the time. We have an image of ourselves and that image is usually portrayed on our faces for all to read. It has taken us years to put this image in our minds, so it will not be an overnight thing to change it ... but remember that TODAY is the FIRST DAY of the REST OF YOUR LIFE ... so it is never to late to start! Even doing one positive thing each day will mean that by the end of the week you have 7 positive things going for you!

Philippians 4: 4-9
Colossians 1: 9-17

Blessings,
Shirley

- *Food for Thought!*

❖ Have an Attitude of Gratitude!

❖ Anger turned inward is depression. Usually we are angry because we feel out of control, frustrated, depressed, rejected, defeated, or misunderstood.

❖ Life is an open book test … so open "The Book" (the Bible) daily!

❖ Rules without relationship lead to rebellion (Josh McDowell)

❖ People don't really care how much you know until they know how much you care.

❖ The middle letter in sin is "I" … interesting! Write down your sin, ask forgiveness, put it in the shredder … God doesn't want you to live in sin.

- *The Weaver*

> *My life is but a weaving*
> > *Between my Lord and me,*
> *I cannot choose the colors*
> > *He worketh steadily*
>
> *Oft times He weaveth sorrow,*
> > *And I in foolish pride*
> *Forget He sees the upper*
> > *And I, the underside.*

Not till the loom is silent
> *And the shuttles cease to fly*
Shall God unroll the canvas
> *And explain the reason why.*

The dark threads are as needful
> *In the Weaver's skillful hand*
As the threads of gold and silver
> *In the pattern He has planned.*

> *Grant Coifax Tullar*

Chapter 6

✓ **<u>Starting A Job Search … Finding A Job</u>**

… "Houston, We've Got A Problem!"

… Ah yes, don't you just cringe when you are called into a conference room or into an office with someone from human resources and you hear those loaded words … that go something like … "We are having a reorganization and consolidation!" Your heart falls out of your chest and wraps itself somewhere around your ankles and you stop breathing for a few seconds as you listen intently in complete silence, praying that this conversation is not being directed at YOU! But alas, it is, and the job you once had … even a moment ago … is now, this instant, no longer yours. So, who needs a paycheck anyway! You think, this must be the twilight zone and this cannot be happening. If you were me, you would be saying not only does it feel like the twilight zone, but it cannot be happening to me, yet again!!! I have experienced this so often you would think I was wearing an invisible sign that says, "If you are having a layoff soon, hire me!" It's rather laughable … it's just not very funny!

If there is time, and you are not "out the door" at that very moment, ask someone who likes you to write you a letter of recommendation, or if they will be a referral for you.

If there is not time and your departure is quick, you could send them an e-mail from home and ask if they would be kind enough to write a letter of recommendation for you. This will go a long way to helping you get your next position.

Okay, first things first. Breath! It may be death of a vision and a job, but there is another one and all you need is one! Trust me; I have been through this soooooooooo many times that I could write the book on it ... or at least a chapter in this book!

In these crazy economic times, sometimes we have to think outside the box, use other resources and lots of networking to find new sources of income. Check to see if any churches in your area sponsor a career network group.

Hopefully when times were good you put away some finances to help when a "rainy day ... or days" came along. Kind of like Noah building the ark while the sun was shining ... We have to plan for rainy days when it is sunny out ... even if people laugh. Make plans for your future ... because we can be sure the rain will come!

✓ Things to Remember When Starting a Job Search:

➢ You are still alive and still have many wonderful gifts and talents.

➢ This may be a good time to assess your gifts and talents to determine if you are in the right field. Perhaps consider checking out other avenues of work.

➢ **<u>Go and sign up for unemployment at your local unemployment office or on-line to help generate some income while you are involved in your job search for your next opportunity.</u>** Remember, you have paid into this system during your years of working, and now it is there to assist you pay some bills during your job search.

➢ Soon your medical insurance will end. **<u>While you still have medical insurance</u>**, think about any prescriptions you may need to refill so you still get the company discount. Also, when was the last time you had a complete physical ... men and ladies... don't forget your yearly exam. Have you seen your dentist in the last 6 months and had your teeth cleaned? How about your eyes, have you had them checked? If you don't take care of you, who else will? Be wise and use your head! Take this opportunity to pick up your phone and make all those appointments today before your insurance runs out!

- Now, take a look at *www.e-insurance.com* on your computer which will be much less expensive than applying for COBRA. They have many different plans to service many different needs. You just have to think about how many times a year you go to see the doctor … a lot or a little … and then make sure you remember to have some insurance in case of an accident and you land in the hospital for a few days. I assure you, it will be a lot less than buying into COBRA. If you have some serious medical issues, you may choose to go with COBRA. However, it's worth checking it out to see which is most cost effective and gives you the doctors and the care you need.

- While you are under some degree of stress processing all of this, don't forget to take your vitamins! If you loose your health … well, that's another story!

- Update your resume. Remember to write a nice cover letter that tells a little about yourself and your interest in your field of work; explain the highlights of your career, your accomplishments and how they may contact you. Attach a letter of recommendation or two, and mention that referrals are available upon request. If spelling and English grammar are not some of your better traits, you will want to have someone read it over and make suggestions so the employer gets a good "First Impression!" Then post it on various websites:

    - ✓ *www.monster.com*
    - ✓ *www.careerbuilder.com*
    - ✓ *www.washingtonpost.com* … *Or your local newspaper*
    - ✓ *www.washingtonrecruiter.com* … *Or your local site*
    - ✓ *www.indeed.com*
    - ✓ *www.craigslist.com*
    - ✓ *www.jobfox.com*

- ✓ *www.nettemps.com*
- ✓ *www.hotjobs.com*
- ✓ *www.dice.com* ... *This site lists government jobs.*
- ✓ *www.usa.gov*

> **Important Key Point:** Many, many, many people upload their resumes every day. Sooooo, if you want employers to be able to find yours and to know that you are still looking, every week or every two weeks, go into each job website where you have posted your resume and **change one thing so that your resume will show that it was "updated" and it will bounce it back up to the top of the list of resumes again!** The easiest thing I have found to change is the way the phone number appears, i.e. you can change it from 701-222-4444 to 701.222.4444 to 701 / 222-4444 to (701) 222-4444. Any little change will result in an "update" and your resume will be back at the top of the list for employers to see. Remember numerous resumes have been posted to the website since you last updated yours! Some of the websites have an edit tab that allows you to update just by clicking on the box.

> Remember to check the box so that employers can view your resume. Then, let the system work for you. Look for e-mails from companies searching for people with your skill set.

> Check the websites daily, or at least 2 to 3 times per week to see what new opportunities are available. Apply for these jobs and pray that your resume, cover letter and letters of recommendation are the ticket for your new opportunity.

> Check with the Temp Agencies in your area as they can often open the door of opportunity for you and the position may become permanent. It's a great way to get to "look inside the company and get a feel for the environment" so that you know if you want this to become a permanent position. Do your best in whatever they ask you to do. Your shining example and attitude may just open other doors!

> Dress for success! Remember: You never get a 2nd chance to make a 1st impression!

After yet another layoff.... I wrote a friend:

Gordon,

The "job hunt" is in progress "again" and I'm "adding more info to my book on the subject" ... sheesh! If there was some kind of award for having the most jobs in any time frame, I think I could win it hands down! The only problem is that the award would probably be something like a head of cabbage ... or maybe a bungee cord for the resilience it takes to keep "beginning again!" Duh! Oh well, I have to chuckle to keep my sense of humor and sanity!

Through some contacts I learned that Volkswagen is moving 400 jobs from Michigan to Herndon in brand new office space, so I have been over there to put my face and personality in front of them... since my resume certainly may not be the ticket! Actually I have packaged it with a cover letter, 3 letters of recommendation, then my resume, then references – in that order! I was also able to visit a couple of other companies with opportunities near the Reston Town Center. Finding a job is a job! Maybe I should become a recruiter! Continuing to praise, pray, listen, hear and work towards a solution.

Thank you for taking the time to listen and laugh with me on Friday. When trials come, they are sometimes easier to work through when you can share them, laugh at them, and gain new strength to forge ahead. Life doesn't always seem to make sense!
Times like this are definitely "character building," as if I didn't have enough character already! Sometimes I just have to laugh at life to release the stress, because the reality of it all is actually not very funny! Sometimes I feel like Jonah. No whale or big fish has tried to swallow me, but I've definitely been tossed overboard! For one motivated, high-energy, creative, people oriented individual, who loves the Lord, figuring it out is all part of the journey!

Times like this cause me to be reflective and remind me that I'm thankful for family, friends, people that love me, my health, knowing that the Lord is my Savior and is not scratching His head ... though I'm scratching mine! I'm thankful I own my home, that I have not spent my last dime, am not in debt and have some resources.

I heard a song this morning that said it well ... "As He is the potter and I am the clay, I pray He will mold me, make me, use me, fill me, talk with me, and walk beside me. I give my life into the potter's hand for His glory and pray that I may see life through His eyes, captivated by His calling."

I choose to seek His face, listen intently to hear His voice, be intentional, and pray for discernment of His will and direction for my life. I continue to remind myself to "praise Him" in the midst of the trial (Philippians 4:6-7). As the Lord brings me to mind, please pray that I would hear His voice! I will continue to pray for you, that the Lord would bring you the right financial person to assist you, and for your clients in this very difficult economy!

Blessings,
Shirley

It's one day at a time and I just wake up each morning, Praise the Lord for a new day, ask Him to guide and direct me, give me wisdom and I put one foot in front of the other.

When I get tired and run out of ideas, I sit in the sun, or clean out the garage or the refrigerator so I can see some progress somewhere!!! I'm human ... and sometimes I just need a good cry, or to curl up in a ball and try to rest. Then I get up again and try to balance creative ideas and things that need to get done. There's no magic. Balance is the key and sometimes I just need a break from the job search. These are some of the things I have done to gain a sense of accomplishment:

- ✓ I've painted a room
- ✓ Cut branches off a couple of bushes
- ✓ Done yard work and pulled weeds
- ✓ Cut back sticker bushes
- ✓ Cleaned out the garage
- ✓ Met friends for lunch
- ✓ Cleaned out closets

- ✓ Sorted papers and clothes
- ✓ Drove to the beach or a local lake to reflect and relax
- ✓ Planted flowers
- ✓ Cleaned shower tiles
- ✓ Re-caulked windows!
- ✓ Had dinner with a friend
- ✓ Gone for a walk
- ✓ Rode my bicycle to see the sites, get outside and breathe fresh air!

I try to turn over every stone I find, walk through every door He puts in front of me, pray God makes the connections and brings forth the fruit from my labors.

Exercise Your Faith: Remember to pray daily and Praise the Lord in the midst of your search. He is not confused or scratching His head. Though you may not have a clue where or how the next employer will come from, begin your walk of faith believing that He will direct. Sometimes out of the blue someone will contact you and tell you about an opening that just happens to be perfect for you! If this happens to you, Praise the Lord! If not, start the process of looking on the internet at job websites, sending out your resume on-line, networking and going to job fairs in your area. Ask the Lord to open windows and doors of opportunity as you do the footwork to lead you to your next job. Ask your friends to pray for you and thank them for their prayers on your behalf.

➢ Philippians 4:6

➢ Isaiah 55

➢ Psalm 27

➢ I can't over emphasize that "Balance is Important!" Determine the best part of your day for work … looking for your next job on the computer, making phone calls and networking, run errands, play, exercise. Keeping a balance in your daily routine will help you keep your sanity!

➤ Networking with those you have previously worked with is a key to finding your next potential opportunity. People know people and former-co-workers may know of something where they are working. Also going to a new activity you would enjoy, or responding to financial seminars where they offer a free dinner for your willingness to listen … provides a nice meal, the opportunity for you to meet people you would otherwise not get to meet, learn and engage your brain in thought provoking activity, and someone there may just know someone who knows someone. Financial planners have many contacts and are a good resource, so take along your resume and letters of recommendation to pass along! You might create a business card with your contact information and the types of work you are seeking so you can give them out to people you meet.

➤ Your list of references and those who have written letters of recommendation for you are also important contacts. Let them know of your situation and availability.

➤ Contact every temporary and employment agency in the area, send them your resume, cover letter and letters of recommendation. I got desperate and even attached my picture to the e-mail that I forwarded to them! It may sound unusual, but if it could enhance your chances of getting an interview, there is no law that says you can't attach a picture! (Note …. Please make sure it is business appropriate!)

➤ Each morning I continued to check the websites to see the new job listings and forwarded my resume, cover letter and letters of recommendation to those opportunities that seemed like a good fit. You can sort the jobs that pop up in date order … that way you are looking at the new job listings first.

➤ Look on the web for Job Fairs or Career Fairs in your area. Just type in job fairs and your city and state. This is where many companies meet at one location and have recruiters available to speak with you. Take many copies of your resume and dress to impress as "you only get one chance to make a good first impression!" Look the part that you want to fill. Dress for success! Don't forget your smile! There may be long lines of people, so plan to be there for 2-3 hours and take along a snack if you are like me and get hungry! A few nuts and raisins will recharge your energy level and give you more stamina.

➢ If you happen to be in the DC area, McLean Bible Church has a Career Network gathering once a week where you can connect with other people experiencing a job change and draw from their experiences. Look for these opportunities local to you.

➢ After you have sent your resume to a variety of potential employers, call and ask to speak to someone in Recruiting. When you speak with someone about the open position, be sure you get their e-mail address and offer to send them your resume! This way it arrives at their desk ... and not just in a pile of resumes received by the company.

➢ If the phone isn't ringing, dress for success, look your best and start visiting the temporary and employment agencies where you sent your resume. This way you are putting a name and a face together for them which can often be the ticket to opening doors for your next job opportunity. Make a good first impression. Remember to SMILE! Shake their hand. Let your face show that you are interested in making a good first impression and present a positive attitude.

➢ Remember, the road to success is always under construction!

➢ And, while you are out visiting the agencies, look at the directory in the lobby of each building you enter! There just might be another employment agency on the list that you were not aware of, or a similar company to those you have worked with before. It never hurts to have extra copies of your cover letter, resume and letters of recommendation with you to hand out to those interested in meeting you! It's only the cost of paper and ink and shoe leather, so go with a smile and a good attitude. Remember you only need one job and you never know which door you open will be the one that offers you the job!

> Networking is always key. Let your friends, neighbors and others that you meet know that you are looking. They may know of an opening in their office.

> Here's a piece of a note I wrote during one of my days of unemployment in response to an encouragement to seek out my passion in life and find a way to incorporate it into my next job opportunity:

My real passion in life has always been to nurture, love and encourage others whether in the role of wife and mother, making a house feel like a home, or creating fun holidays and events. Being on Young Life staff, working with teenagers, helping to draw them out, and being the conduit between them, their parents and understanding God's word was an awesome chapter of my life. I continue to reach out to neighbors, co-workers, friends and people I don't even know... yet. Administrative, creative, marketing, sales, great aromas coming from the kitchen and "going fishing" to draw people out are a by-product of gifts and talents in my DNA which I have nurtured over the years, as well as my love for the Lord and desire to serve and honor Him in whatever I do. Somehow all of that needs to be channeled into something I can actually get paid for!

I tend to run "high-energy" and enjoy a challenge, especially if it's something I feel like I have the ability to accomplish ... even if it causes me to fry a few brain cells in the process!

In addition to uploading my info on Monster, CareerBuilder, Indeed Job Alert (alert@indeed.com), WashingtonPost.com and tracking their leads, I've been wearing out the soles on my shoes networking, visiting agencies and companies putting a name and face together marketing my skills in hopes of a lead that will open a door. God calls us to walk by faith (Hebrews 11:6) and not by sight. It is easy to loose sight of God's perspective and become fearful, anxious and discouraged! Sunday morning as part of Lon's sermon (McLean Bible Church), he said: "God is bigger than all your obstacles!" (Well that's reassuring!)

In the Old Testament, even though the report came back that there were walled cities, big armies and giants in the land, Caleb went forth believing that God had already given him the city (Numbers 13:30). If you want the fruit, sometimes you have to be intentional and go out on the limb where it grows!

✓ <u>**Have you thought about spending time with entrepreneurs that have the knowledge to teach you how to grow your own business?**</u>

- Consider going to a meeting and learning more. You may just discover you have a way to build your own business at very little cost (under $100) and reap the rewards, plus get the tax advantages. The nice thing about these companies is that you don't need a "degree in anything" … all you need is "a desire to try" to qualify! You will get on the job training and counseling! *<u>Introducing Mangosteen – "The Queen of Fruits!"</u>* You may visit my website at *www.sonshine.mymangosteen.com* to learn more about this opportunity or contact me at: *win4him7@gmail.com* . You will find further information at *www.pubmed.com* where you can search for Mangosteen and _____ … whatever physical ailment you may have and see what research has been done at National Institutes of Health (NIH).

✓ Being prepared for that Job Interview

- Check the website and know a few facts about the company where you are interviewing. They will be impressed that you took the time to check them out and it allows you to learn a few facts so you will sound informed, somewhat knowledgeable and intelligent during the interview! I also tend to be an "eagle eye" proofreader … which means I read slowly and find most mistakes. I'm not the kind of person who will ever read a 400 page book, but I would be high on your list for spell-check! Therefore, I read with my "eagle eye" when checking out a company's website and circle any errors … not to be offensive, but to show a skill. They are always anxious to have their web person correct any errors so they present well on their webpage!

- Have you thought of a few key questions to ask during your interview? It's always good to have some basic questions as it shows that you have interest in their company and what they are looking for in a candidate. I've attached the questionnaire that I have created and used successfully. You might pick out 2 or 3 questions from the list to ask each person with whom you interview. I wouldn't ask all of the questions to any one person.

✓ **Job Interview Questionnaire ... Form Attached in the Appendix** ... After you have looked at their company website, print out a page or two, highlight a few key facts, then look through the list of questions and decide on a few to ask to help you be confident and go in prepared.

- Note: This is great to use when you have a phone interview as well. It helps you remember what they said when you have your face-to-face interview and you are ready to choose a few others questions from the list that are yet unanswered. It is a tool to help you come across as confident, organized and sharp!

A caterpillar doesn't change into a butterfly overnight ... but this could be the season to start fresh and recreate yourself. You have a blank canvas, go paint your world!!! Think outside the box and expand your horizons so you can begin to fly again!

❋ ~ ❋ ~ ❋

Chapter 7

✓ **<u>Success</u>**

- *What is your definition of success?*

Some think it is obtaining things, financial freedom, helping those less fortunate?

When it is all said and done and you breathe your last breath ... what will have been important to you? If someone were to look at your checkbook, look at your family and talk to your co-workers, what would they reveal? Did you leave a legacy that causes you to rest well after a job well done? Did you lean your ladder of success on the right wall? Will you wish you had spent more time at the office, or will you realize that the children you gave life to need you at each stage of their growth. Guys - your spouse needs to know that you love her and that she is needed and cherished? Gals – your husband needs to know you respect him for the many ways he cares for you and your family, and the many things he does so well.

- *Love Languages ... Success in communicating with those you love*

Have you ever noticed that all the cards at the store talk about "love" (which is a woman's heart language), and it is very rare if ever that you will find one that says "respect" (which is a man's mother tongue)! To better understand this, check out Chapter 9 and read Emerson Eggerich's book Love & Respect. Better yet, view the DVD as Emerson is quite animated and knows how to help you understand this topic in a whole new light. It is truly a light bulb moment!

In the book To a Child LOVE is Spelled T-I-M-E, Lance Wubbels tell the story of an old man who went looking for a photograph in the attic. While searching he came across a journal from his grown son's childhood. Opening it his eyes brightened as he read words penned by a six-year old that spoke to his soul and their magic carried him back in time. He wondered how different his own journal read on that day and went to his den to read what he had logged for that day. The old man read his brief description of the day where he had penned "Wasted the whole day fishing with Jimmy. Didn't catch a thing." With a sigh he took Jimmy's journal and looked at his son's entry for the same day. In large scrawling letters it read, "Went fishing with my Dad. Best day of my life." Only then did he realize that his son's simple recollections of those days were far different from his own.

Have you learned to speak the "love language" of those you care about? What is your love language? Learn about different love languages in The Five Love Languages by Gary Chapman, and Gary Smalley & John Trent, Ph.D. in their book The Language of Love. How can you change things so that your epitaph says something you are proud of because you know you took the time to care and make a difference? Are you leaving a heritage to pass down to your children that gives you peace of mind of a job well done? Remember, there will not be a U-Haul following your hearse down the street to your grave.

Maybe it's time to do a "self-assessment" and ask yourself (as Morgan Freeman asks in *The Bucket List*) ...

- ❖ Have you found joy in your life?

- ❖ Has your life brought joy to others?

- *Intentionally Desire to Serve One Another ...*

When her children were small, my sister Sue started a tradition in their home. During the Christmas holiday she would place the manger scene on the coffee table with Mary and Joseph, the 3 wise men, the animals, and the basket for baby Jesus. The straw to fill the basket was set on the table. Each time someone did something nice for someone else, often times without the receiver knowing who did such a nice thing, the person who did the giving put a piece of straw into the basket to prepare for Jesus' coming. By Christmas day, there was a nice bed of straw awaiting the arrival of baby Jesus. This example can be used year round as you "intentionally desire to serve one another," and take the initiative to bless one another in ways you know will be appreciated by the recipient. Remember, "Don't save it all for Christmas," but rather enjoy the joy of giving all year round!

- *How To Forgive (WOW!) ... Author Unknown*

One day a while back, a man, his heart heavy with grief, was walking in the woods. As he thought about his life this day, he knew many things were not right. He thought about those who had lied about him back when he had a job.

His thoughts turned to those who had stolen his things and cheated him.

He remembered family that had passed on. His mind turned to the illness he had that no one could cure. His very soul was filled with anger, resentment and frustration.

Standing there this day, searching for answers he could not find, knowing all else had failed him, he knelt at the base of an old oak tree to seek the One he knew would always be there. And with tears in his eyes, he prayed:

"Lord, You have done wonderful things for me in this life. You have told me to do many things for you, and I happily obeyed. Today, you have told me to forgive. I am sad, Lord, because I cannot. I don't know how. It is not fair Lord. I didn't deserve these wrongs that were done against me and I shouldn't have to forgive.

As perfect as your way is Lord, this one thing I cannot do, for I don't know how to forgive. My anger is so deep Lord, I fear I may not hear you, but I pray that you teach me to do this one thing I cannot do - Teach me To Forgive."

As he knelt there in the quiet shade of that old oak tree, he felt something fall onto his shoulder. He opened his eyes. Out of the corner of one eye, he saw something red on his shirt.

He could not turn to see what it was because where the oak tree had been was a large square piece of wood in the ground. He raised his head and saw two feet held to the wood with a large spike through them.

He raised his head more, and tears came to his eyes as he saw Jesus hanging on a cross. He saw spikes in His hands, a gash in His side, a torn and battered body, deep thorns sunk into His head. Finally he saw the suffering and pain on His precious face. As their eyes met, the man's tears turned to sobbing, and Jesus began to speak.

"Have you ever told a lie?" He asked.
The man answered - "Yes, Lord."

"Have you ever been given too much change and kept it?"
The man answered - "Yes, Lord." And the man sobbed more and more.

"Have you ever taken something from work that wasn't yours?" Jesus asked.
And the man answered - "Yes, Lord."

"Have you ever sworn, using my Father's name in vain? "
The man, crying now, answered - "Yes, Lord."

As Jesus asked many more times, "Have you ever...?" The man's crying became uncontrollable, for he could only answer - "Yes, Lord."

Then Jesus turned His head from one side to the other, and the man felt something fall on his other shoulder. He looked and saw that it was the blood of Jesus. When he looked back up, his eyes met those of Jesus, and there was a look of love the man had never seen or known before.

Jesus said, "I didn't deserve this either, but I forgive you."

When you truly ask forgiveness, remember to leave the weight of the burden with your creator, God Almighty who created the heavens and the earth, the stars, the ocean, the birds of the air and the fish of the sea, and He created you. Close the door on that chapter of your life and choose to live for a higher calling and purpose. Do not let the past define you future. If God is smiling at you, why are you tap-dancing for anyone else? A bird sings because he has a song to sing, not because he has to sing. Think about it and learn to walk into your future with a new lease on life, new perspective, new desire, new thinking. Each day God gives you a new blank canvas. Go paint your world and make a difference. As you find ways to make someone else's life better, you will reap the benefits. Try it and see.

Hate is more toxic than any acid and it will eat you up. Think about it ... who does it hurt ... you or the one you hate. Forgiveness is a sign of strength and frees you to live again. God is much better able to bring them to their knees than you will ever know. Work at being the person God wants you to be. Who you are and what you do matters to God. This is not a dress rehearsal. Tell God what's on your heart, where you have failed and ask forgiveness. He will help to lead you out and through your situation. He is listening.

Remember ... Sometimes the act of forgiving is not something that you do for the other person, it is something you do for yourself!

- ***Keys to Healthy Communication***

❖ Ask questions instead of making statements.

❖ <u>Use "I" statements instead or "YOU" statements.</u>

- ✓ "I" statements express your feelings and concerns.

  - "Did I say something disrespectful (stepped on your air hose) that made you feel unloved?"
  - "Did I come across unloving and make you feel disrespected?"
  - "I was wrong. Will you forgive me?" The "more mature" person in any relationship will be the first to take ownership for their actions and ask forgiveness if another has been offended.

- ✓ "You" statements express pointed positive or negative comments … and often put the other person on the defensive which may close down communication or cause flare-ups!

❖ Avoid saying the words *"Always" and "Never."*

❖ Realize that we may not "know all the facts … even though we may think we do!"

  - ✓ Say: *"Let me repeat back to you what I think I heard you say."*
  - ✓ Then: *Allow the other person to fill in the "puzzle pieces you are missing!"*
  - ✓ If a puzzle has 12 pieces and you are making decisions not realizing you only have 9 of the pieces … the outcome of your thinking will be inaccurate.
  - ✓ Give the other person a chance to openly share their thoughts, concerns, desires.

❖ Be willing to *"Love the other person in A Way that is Meaningful to them,"* which may be 180 degrees different from something that would be meaningful to you.

  - ✓ Listen and learn what is important to them.
  - ✓ Stop … and Think About: What are their goals and dreams? What is important to them?
  - ✓ Think About: What would make them happy … versus what would make me happy.
  - ✓ If you don't know what would please them and make them happy … ASK … Then listen to their responses … Then Take ACTION and Actually "Do It!"

- An example of this happened to me recently. There were 3 of us on a round water raft with friends in a lake. A 6 ft guy of about 170+ lbs stood up on the edge of the vinyl raft ... and you can guess what happened. Immediately we flew into the water. I suppose he was just clowning around and thought it was funny. However when I surfaced I had water up into my sinuses, I wasn't sure if I still had both contacts and well, forget the hair style!

- When I was silent, others asked if I was okay. My response was that I wasn't planning to get my hair wet, I wasn't sure if I still had both contacts due to the rush of water in my face and my sinuses were still adjusting.

- His response was that he didn't know it would tip! That type of comment is an insult to my intelligence and comes across childlike.

  - It takes no responsibility for what happened
  - It tries to cover up the incident as no fault on his part
  - It has no concern for how another might feel
  - It doesn't move the conversation towards resolution
  - Later he said, "I like your hair."

- Truthfully, I didn't care if he liked my hair or not. It would have been much more appropriate if he would have moved the conversation off himself and his feelings and said something that showed he cared about my feelings, i.e. "I wasn't thinking about your hair, your contacts or water rushing up your nose. I'm sorry." That type of response opens the door to communication, forgiveness and reconciliation.

❖ <u>*Tone of Voice is More Important Than You May Realize*</u> ... It will either help people to listen to what you are saying or turn a deaf ear. How you say what you say is So Very Important if you want a positive response. People are often willing to listen if they feel they are not being "talked down to."

❖ **REMEMBER** … Before reacting to a statement or comment … be willing to say to the other person: *"Let me tell you what I think I heard you say."* After sharing, allow the other person to respond and fill in the missing pieces to express what they were trying to convey.

- *Four Rules for Good Communication*

    1. *Be Honest*   -   Ephesians 4:25
    2. *Keep Current*   -   Ephesians 4:26
    3. *Attack Problems Not People* -   Ephesians 4:29
    4. *Act … Not React*   -   Ephesians 4:31-21

Do what is necessary … Do what is possible … Be faithful … Let God do the miracle!

Jim & Marty Hartman raised six boys who now have families of their own. Jerry and Becky Hartman (their son and daughter-in-law), along with Jim & Marty Hartman were a wonderful, nurturing Christian influence on my son, Josh, during the season of time he lived in their lovely home in North Carolina. They provided wisdom, grace, and warm fellowship in a time of need. The ladies made some memorable meals that Josh and Caleb and many others enjoyed. Jerry (Coach) lead Bible Studies with the students at Campbell University and invited the guys to their home. Jim is a wonderful grandpa who reminds us to keep these things in mind as you are dealing with any situation:

- Develop Wise Planning – Get Counsel
- Use Common Sense
- Keep abreast of the facts!
- Pray and ask for guidance

Kim,

It was great to get to spend some time catching up while driving together!!! Thanks for being my GPS to get us safely to our destination. Once I figured out how to communicate with my GPS, I was on my way home. My GPS and I are "slowly" becoming friends ... and if I would take the time to sit down and actually read the book, it might help a good bit!!! Ha!

While driving and reflecting on some things, it occurred to me that as our kids are "leaving the nest," you may want to find a time each week to think and talk about the following items:

- ✓ *Dreams .... What were they years ago and what are they now?*

- ✓ *Hopes .... Life has a way of passing us by and sometimes things we dreamed and hoped for often seem somehow out of reach.*

- ✓ *When the kids start to leave home, it is not unusual to reflect on the years gone by and ask ourselves ... So, what's it all about anyway? Where are we? How did we get here? Where are we going?*

- ✓ *Time is a fleeting thing that no one can harness, and sometimes whether we know it or not, we find ourselves waking up one day and feeling out of control. It can be a scary thought. Sometimes we can feel like we are in a mid-life crisis. We can't control:*

  - ➢ *How old we are and how we look older as we look into the mirror*
  - ➢ *The hair we are loosing*
  - ➢ *Our health issues*
  - ➢ *Our shattered dreams*
  - ➢ *Our ability to accomplish what we thought we would have by now*

- ✓ *It's important to talk through our feelings as they are the things that deep down drive our emotions and either bring us the feeling of great satisfaction ... or the desire to want to burst wide-open because we can't deal with all that's been bottled up inside.*

- ✓ *Often going to the Christian book store, checking out their recommendation on a good book on Communication ... and setting aside maybe an hour on a Sunday afternoon to read it together will open amazing communication.*

- ➢ *Find a time that works well for both of you and make it a date.*

- ➢ *Women usually have to remind their men each week that you get together because women are built with the DNA to desire to communicate.*

- ➢ *Men are wired very differently, so don't be disappointed if he shows initial lack of interest.*

- ➢ *Keep it on your calendars and mention how much it means to you to take this time to reflect and continue building your communication.*

- ➢ *Make it fun. Make a picnic and take it to the park or sit by a waterfall. Or at home, make popcorn and sit by the fireplace where it is a warm and inviting atmosphere.*

- ➢ *Whether you read a few paragraphs, a few pages or the whole chapter, the length is not as important as stopping when something strikes your heart and brings up something important to talk about. Keep at it each week and you will reap the benefits!*

✓ *Plans for the future ... Begin to think ahead 5 years and what you want it to look like. How will you spend your time?*

Ah, the adventure is just beginning and sometimes we just have to fan the flame in the right direction to get the embers warm again before the stresses of life try to snuff them out.

Praying God's best for you and His intervention to bless you with the joy of what He can do when you build some bridges to your future.

Love, hugs and prayers,
Shirley

✵ ~ ✝ ~ ✵

Chapter 8

✓ **<u>Counseling – Uncle Earl … Truths that Transform</u>**

Soon after we moved from Maryland to Pennsylvania for my husband to attend Westminster Seminary, Jack's daughter Wendy called and told her dad that she wanted to come to live with him as things were not going well with her mom. He immediately said yes and told me about the decision. I became an instant step-mother of a 10 year old little girl. That's a whole story which I will not attempt to unpack here, other than to say that year's later (when Jack wanted a divorce) counselors assured me that making such a decision without consulting your spouse is not a marriage. Marriage is a team effort and both parents (step or biological) need to be on board with the decision of bringing a child into your home as well as structure and discipline if the marriage is to survive.

Wendy had low self-esteem, couldn't smile naturally, and was getting very poor grades at school. She had spent long hours with babysitters who let her watch TV while her mom worked long hours at a law office. With no one to lovingly nurture her and encourage her to apply herself, she was in a downward spiral. Needless to say, our mostly harmonious little apartment quickly became one of chaos, disorder and stress.

I knew we were in trouble and sought out help at the Westminster Seminary Counseling Center. This is where we were introduced to "Uncle Earl" who was a delightful, warm, welcoming grandfather type individual who did miracles in our lives in 6 weeks by teaching us *principles* to put into place in our home! His years of knowledge, his love for the Lord and Godly perspective, as well as his humor and ability to work with children were a true gift. Uncle Earl was a wonderful counselor and I was and am still truly amazed at the transformation that took place when Wendy knew there was weekly accountability to a third party! Kids may take you on as parents, but there is a different element that is introduced when you add a counselor that they will see each week. We met with Uncle Earl every week at a given time and were to report in on the past week. We were then given *guidelines* on how to proceed for the next week. Amazingly, as we progressed and put these **simple yet profound principles** into practice, we saw major changes occur. The yelling stopped. Wendy began to blossom and her self-image rose to new heights. Her grades improved and she began to smile naturally. Praise the Lord!!!

Whether your children are young or older, know that you have the power to say, **"I have learned that I have not been using the right tools for our family and I apologize to you and ask your forgiveness."** Children do not come with an instruction book on how to handle every circumstance. However, God's word does give us Godly principles to help create harmony and structure in our home. You may not always get it right, but keep working at these principles and learn to use these new guidelines.

You can say to your family, *"Now that I am aware of these principles, this day we as a family are going to start living with principles that work. This will be a team effort and as we all learn to work this "game of life" for the good of our family, there will be consequences and rewards. It can be great fun, or it can be painful. The choice is yours! (Know that kids generally love a game and a challenge!) Our goal is to see a miracle with transformed lives, harmony in our home, improved self-image, new perspective and to restore or find a love and respect for one another that should have been here from the start."*

Here are some of the principles Uncle Earl taught us to put into action to regain harmony in our home:

<u>Principles for Harmony in Our Home ... A Home That Honors God ... (List of Family Rules with Consequences) – No Yelling Zone:</u>

Out of frustration and lack of tools, many parents come to the end of their wits and let off steam in the form of harsh words. Jack would get so frustrated as Wendy had learned to lie to cover up whenever it was convenient. In order to put a stop to the yelling, we were encouraged to make a list of the "house rules" and Wendy was to make her own list of what she thought to be the "house rules" which included simple things like make your bed, brush your teeth, do your homework, tell the truth, etc. Then we were to create a column next to each of these with a consequence if they were not accomplished. What we discovered that was most interesting was that the counselor had the parents create one list and the child created her own list. Sometimes the punishments the child suggested were tougher than the parents had noted. Then we came together and with the help of the counselor decided on what the final list would say and it was then posted on her bedroom door.

There was to be no yelling. We were assured that the rules would definitely be tested many, many, many times during the week to see if we meant business. And so they were tested many times each day, and our role was to say, "Go look at your list and tell us what needs to happen." No yelling or disappointment on the part of the parents, just matter-of-factly stating, "Go look at your list." The following week we were to report back to the counselor as to how we were doing. It's amazing what a little pressure from the right source and accountability will do! Things started to change and she became a much happier child! Taking on responsibility for what one needs to do builds one's self-image and an authentic smile began to emerge. Delightful ... absolutely delightful ... the fruit of our labors was beginning to blossom. Praise the Lord!!!

Know that children often do bad things to get attention. When you don't react negatively, it takes the zest out of the game. As parents, learn to give your child positive attention and compliments for things they do right! On a daily basis, stop long enough to take notice and look for little things to praise them and give them compliments. Often times giving them positive attention fills their love tank so they don't have to resort to negative actions to get you to notice them. To a child, time and positive attention spells LOVE.

The "I Lost It Box!" … $ … A Verse to Memorize: Ah, yes, what an ingenious idea! The reality is that too many things get left out and not put away. Both parents and children were to play this little game and we were all to learn together. The idea for this game is that when the child / children go to bed, all of their things must be put away, including shoes, books, coats, toys, etc. Anything that is left out of place went into the "I Lost It Box" until a designated day and time each week when it could be removed … after paying a small fee depending on the age of the child (from 5 cents to 25 cents to 50 cents to $1.00). Also, when the children woke up in the morning, they were allowed to put items into the box that the parents had left out and it cost the parents $1.00 to $5.00 per item. Both child and parent were required to memorize the verse chosen for that week before removing their items. We were warned that one mother used to leave her shoes all over the house and the child put them all in the box. Learning to change old habits takes time for everyone, but they began to see progress!!!

Calendar and Stars: I discovered the use of a calendar and stars provides great motivation for a child! As you set up guidelines as to basic things that need to happen around your household, have the child help determine the list of items that need to be accomplished on a daily basis, i.e. make your bed, brush your teeth, eat your meals, put away your things, do your homework, etc. and with a good attitude! Place your list on their door so it is easily visible and use pictures if they can't read words. If things are accomplished all morning with a good attitude, they get a star for the morning. The same is true if things go well in the afternoon, then they get another star on the same day! Establish that by the end of the week if they have stars for morning and afternoon there will be a "surprise" on (pick the day) Saturday or Sunday. It may be breakfast with Dad at McDonalds, a walk in the park, a visit to the pet shop to play with the puppies, a visit to the nursing home to encourage older folks, a game of baseball with them and their friends, cooking in the kitchen with mom, a treat you know they will like. Motivation instills action and action gets things done and builds good habits!

The Sandwich Approach: We've all heard that a little bit of sugar helps the medicine go down. …. So remember to use that approach when teaching a truth or trying to get your point across. An honest compliment always builds up one's self-esteem and lets a child or adult know that you appreciate them as a person. Sometimes asking a question with a positive attitude will help stir the memory of the person you are speaking with to encourage them to take care of a needed task. If not, you may have to be more direct and let them know the time slot when something needs to be done. If still no action is taken, then there may need to be a consequence if X is not taken care of by a certain time. Then, when it is accomplished thank them not only for the deed done, but hopefully also for the quality of the work performed.

- **_Other Resources_** …

✓ **_The New Dare to Discipline_** by Dr. James Dobson of Focus on the Family. Self-control, human kindness, respect, and peacefulness can again be manifest in America if we will **dare to discipline** in our homes and schools. Children need love, hugs, trust, healthy affection, hearing the words "I Love You," and appropriate discipline when needed. Children should be able to sense they are Loved by "Your Actions," and your actions should speak louder than "Your Words." From one generation to the next, the challenge of helping children grow into responsible adults doesn't change. Dr. Dobson's classic *Dare to Discipline,* a practical, reassuring guide for caring parents, has sold over 2 million copies since its release in 1970. What gives a book that kind of staying power? The ability to meet a real, felt need in the marketplace. Today, a whole new generation of parents is turning to Dr. Dobson's wise counsel. Some things never change.

✓ **_The Total Transformation Program_** created by behavioral therapist James Lehman. Do you struggle with your child's behavior? Do the research and find out the cause, the solution and how to make tomorrow different from today. **http://www.thetotaltransformation.com**

- ***Have a New Kid by Friday*** ... child psychologist, Dr. Kevin Leman, gives humorous, insightful and effective advice on many behavioral problems for every childhood age and stage.

- <u>*See additional resources in Chapters 7, 9 and 15*</u>

~ † ~

Chapter 9

- ✓ **Life Lessons …**

  - ❖ *Pink & Blue Sunglasses:* Women see life through pink sunglasses and men see life through blue sunglasses. Women have pink air hoses and men have blue air hoses. God made us uniquely different and the person who takes the time to understand the differences will have a much better understanding of how the other thinks and many more tools in their communication tool box which will result in healthy communication and healthy relationships. I highly recommend the DVD entitled *"Love & Respect"* by Emerson Eggerichs. You will laugh and laugh, understand yourself better, understand others in a whole new way and the "light bulb will go on" as to why people struggle to communicate. Emerson has truly "cracked the communication code!!!" Understand why when she feels unloved she acts disrespectful, and why when he feels disrespected he acts unloving. Emerson rightfully calls it "The Crazy Cycle!" Discover how to stop it from spinning"!!!

  Everyone needs to feel respected … and if you learn to speak a man's mother tongue of "Respect," you will fill his blue airhose! Have you ever noticed that our society is so "love" oriented (check the card industry and any woman's heart), that we have forgotten that above the need for love, the honor code among men is "respect."

God's word speaks about this in Ephesians 5 and we as a society have watered it down to the extent that we are in a fog and think wrongly that a man's "mother tongue" should be the same as a woman's. Wrong.

Sue,

It was great seeing you on Sunday and hearing about your engagement!!! What a blessing! You give me hope!!!

I was thinking more about our conversation on how to emulate guys, build up their self-esteem and speak their "mother tongue." As this is somewhat foreign to the female gender, I put together a list of possible phrases for us women to share at the right moment with the men in our lives to show them "RESPECT." We definitely need to practice because it has become a lost art and we all know "these phrases do not come naturally!" How has society missed this for so many years??? Soooooooooo, here's a beginning list and I hope you will add to it since you seem to have mastered this "new language that we women need to learn how to speak!"

- ✓ *I want you to know I "appreciate" you for the way you ………*
- ✓ *I so "appreciate" your thoughtfulness when you ……*
- ✓ *I "admire" you for the way you ………..*
- ✓ *I "admire" your sense of humor and the way you make people feel comfortable*
- ✓ *I "respect" you so much every time I see you take time out to …………..*
- ✓ *My "respect" grows towards you every time I see you work through tough situations. It takes a real man's man to handle things the way you do.*
- ✓ *I "respect" the way you ………*
- ✓ *I "respect" your opinion about ….. and am thankful for the way you think through a situation before reacting.*
- ✓ *I enjoy being with you because I "respect" the way you ………..*
- ✓ *It brings me "great joy to spend time with you" because when I'm with you I feel ……..*

Put on your thinking cap and think about what would speak volumes to your man!

Now, the next question is where are the men that we would like to speak these words to????

Hum, there seems to be a shortage of awesome guys around ... but maybe that's because they have been beaten down, need someone to emulate them, respect them and fill up their "blue air hose" more often!!!

Hugs & blessings,
Shirley

Shirley,

WOW you are on a GREAT Roll!

I especially like: It brings me "great joy to spend time with you" because when I'm with you I feel ....(protected and supported as a possible ending).

The next step I took in learning the language was not to be selective about who receives the language of respect. (I would just cast these seeds LAVISHLY everywhere just for fun). It is really kind of easy for us as females because we only have to remember a few words like respect, admire, strength, honor, appreciate, protect. Then you just look for an opportunity to work these words into the conversation. These statements must come across as being a sincere complement with no strings attached, or else we can be perceived as phony and manipulative.

I would use these words on any male with whom I came in contact, including a 4 year old boy. I figured it was good practice for me, so I could be "fluent" in the language when I had the perfect opportunity.

Speaking of a great opportunity, thank you for serving at the Men's Breakfast and encouraging other ladies to do the same! This is a Brilliant place to practice!

I just practiced and practiced for fun to see what would happen. I made it a contest for me to see who can I bless today and how much can I bless them in their language (not mine). It did not matter what they looked like, how old they were or whether or not I was interested in them as a potential date.

I did have the non-verbal communication to let them know I was only there to bless them for that moment, and it was not an invitation. You have to be careful about this. We can talk about this on the phone rather than via email where things can get confused.

It has been my experience when I started to speak the language of respect (just so I could bless people for fun) there was no shortage of men who would surround me. God brought me lots and lots of men once I started speaking their language and stopped looking for someone for me. It may be that you might step out of the "church box." Lee and I talk about this all the time and disagree. I can tell you more on the phone. Women can call men to a higher place then they are already. Men are hungry for this.

More life changing books for me were:

<u>*How to Get a Date Worth Keeping*</u> *by Dr. Henry Cloud who wrote a variety of books on Boundaries.*

<u>*Captivating*</u> *- John and Staci Eldredge. He also wrote "Wild at Heart." "Captivating" is the woman's version of this.*

If I had not read these books and tried to apply them I would never know Lee.

Congratulations on being such a great Mom! "No good tree bears bad fruit."

Blessings,
Sue

Sue,

Awesome comments! You're right, it will be fun to "practice" this newly discovered language with the right intent and sincerity and see where it goes!

I have both of the books you mention ... though I haven't read all of them. So, at least I'm headed in the right direction!!! I try to go new places and try new things because "the church box" doesn't always attract the type of guy I am looking for ... though for sure he needs to have a growing walk with the Lord. I go dancing and meet a bunch of guys, but no one so far that I'm really attracted to. I've thought about taking up the game of tennis, hanging around boat docks, or trying my hand at golf. Someone even suggested visiting Starbucks or Panera Bread where people tend to "hang out!" And, Yes, the Men's Breakfast ... what a delightful opportunity to "serve" and I shall practice while I'm there!!!

I think I understand what you mean about blessing them for the moment and not creating a situation where you are inviting them for something more. Ah, yes, we must be careful that they don't get the wrong idea since we are using their "mother tongue!" A pleasant smile and a sincere comment should work.

If our society would learn this new language, it will benefit all humanity!

Thank you my friend!

Shirley

Shirley,

You Go girl!

I found I did my best evangelizing during conversations on the dance floor.

It is ok to practice dating with someone you are interested in (just for the sake of practice). This concept comes from How to Get a Date Worth Keeping. I have always been awkward around men. Practice dating was a novel concept to me and it prepared me not to be so nervous when I went out with someone I actually liked.

It also helped me manage my own dating expectations. Enjoy our practice exercises!

Sue

- ❖ *Love Languages – Do You Know Yours?* Gary Chapman has a winsome way of adding additional tools to your toolbox for figuring out relationships and what makes them work in his book <u>**The Five Love Languages**</u>. Gary Smalley & John Trent wrote <u>**The Language of Love**</u> which is an "eye opener" if you think everyone feels loved the same way. As you read and figure out your own love language, you will also easily figure out the love languages of those you love. The key is that they will start to really "feel loved by you" as you better understand how they are wired. Everyone has different DNA and how their personal wiring is designed in their brain gives off very different signals to stimuli. Figuring this out is worth a mint to those you want to express love and concern for and they will truly "feel loved by you." Now that's worth a mint.

- ❖ *God's Word*, the Bible, is a cleansing agent. Reading it helps us realize who we are in His creation, why He created us and specific directions for living life to the fullest with His blessing. The Bible provides correction when we like sheep go astray, restoration when we ask forgiveness and TURN to follow His way, giving praise for His majesty and intricate creation.

Just look around you – did you separate the water from the land, the sky from the ocean, or keep the stars and planets in perfect rotation to provide life on planet earth. Did you set gravity in motion, put all the necessary ingredients in a seed to make it mature and grow year after year and produce new fruit, or create the beauty of the mountains and the variety of fish in the sea. He made the untold number of species of flowers that adorn the earth for your enjoyment, and look at you ... you are one of His creations – different than anyone else from your fingerprints to your likes and dislikes and your outlook on life. Your DNA is different from everyone else! Now that is a miracle in itself! If you disagree, take a look at the enormous detail that goes into your DNA chain and it will leave you speechless!

CHAPTER 9 • 81

You medical, and non-medical, folks - if you haven't already seen this, you will love it!

This is very interesting and something that few of us know. I received this in an e-mail and the author is unknown. It just said ... From a Doctor and Molecular Biologist ...
<u>God's Glue Literally Holds Us Together!</u>

A couple of days ago I was running (I use that term very loosely) on my treadmill, watching a DVD sermon by Louie Giglio... And I was BLOWN AWAY! I want to share what I learned.... But I fear not being able to convey it as well as I want. I will share anyway.

Louie was talking about how inconceivably BIG our God is... How He spoke the universe into being... How He breathes stars out of His mouth that are huge raging balls of fire... Etc., Etc. Then He went on to speak of how this star-breathing, universe creating God ALSO knitted our human bodies together with amazing detail and wonder. At this point I am LOVING it (fascinating from a medical standpoint, you know). And I was remembering how I was constantly amazed during medical school as I learned more and more about God's handiwork. I remember so many times thinking.... 'How can ANYONE deny that a Creator did all of this???'

Louie went on to talk about how we can trust that the God who created all this, also has the power to hold it all together when things seem to be falling apart ... how our loving Creator is also our sustainer.

And then I lost my breath. And it wasn't because I was running on my treadmill, either!!! It was because he started talking about laminin. I knew about laminin. Here is how Wikipedia describes them: 'Laminins are a family of proteins that are an integral part of the structural scaffolding of basement membranes in almost every animal tissue.' You see.... Laminins are what hold us together.... LITERALLY. They are cell adhesion molecules. They are what holds one cell of our bodies to the next cell. Without them, we would literally fall apart. And I knew all this already. But what I didn't know is what they LOOKED LIKE.

But now I do. Here is what the structure of laminin looks like... AND THIS IS NOT a "Christian portrayal" of it.... If you look up laminin in any scientific/medical piece of literature, this is what you will see...

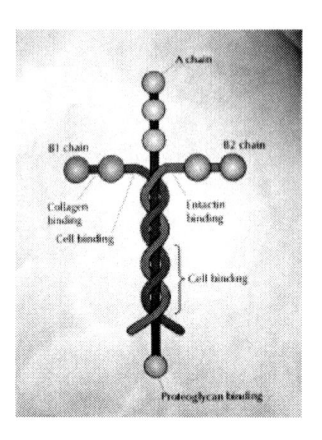

Now tell me that our God is not the coolest!!! Amazing.
The glue that holds us together.... ALL of us.... Is in the shape of the cross.
Immediately Colossians 1:15-17 comes to mind.

"He is the image of the invisible God, the firstborn over all creation.
For by him all things were created; things in heaven and on earth, visible
And invisible, whether thrones or powers or rulers or authorities;
All things were created by him and for him.
He is before all things, and in him
All things HOLD TOGETHER." Colossians 1:15-17

Call me crazy. I just think that is very, very, very cool. Thousands of years before the world knew anything about laminin, Paul penned those words. And now we see that from a very LITERAL stanpoint, **we are held together... One cell to another... By the cross.**

You would never in a quadrillion years convince me that is anything other than the mark of a Creator who knew EXACTLY what laminin 'glue' would look like long before Adam breathed his first breath!!

You will be amazed and enjoy viewing the following video by Louie Giglio as he explains about laminin, which literally holds us together. **http://www.tangle.com/view_video?viewkey=152b5103d741aca61093**

- Don't miss out on the joy as you sense His presence in your life, and the gift of eternally living with Him. When all is said and done and you stand before His throne, you will want to hear Him say, "Well done my child, welcome into My kingdom." Let Him make you the person He designed you to be. God's Word is a lamp to your feet and a light to your path. Walk in His Spirit and it will be as if you are plugged into a wall socket. He will be the energy source that propels you in His power for His glory.

    - *"For in Him all things were created, both in the heavens and on earth, visible and invisible, whether thrones or dominions or rulers or authorities – all things have been created through Him and for Him. And He is before all things, and in Him all things hold together." Colossians 1:16-17*

- *When you start to feel down on yourself .... Are You Going to Finish Strong?* Check out Nick Vujicic's website and the following videos. You will be encouraged!

    http://www.maniacworld.com/are-you-going-to-finish-strong.html

    http://www.tangle.com/view_video?viewkey=18d5fe4e6dcf04df1865

- God calls us to be "Salt & Light" as stated so well in Matthew 5:13-16. "You are the salt of the earth; but if the salt has become tasteless, how will it be made salty again? It is good for nothing any more, except to be thrown out and trampled under foot by men. You are the light of the world. A city set on a hill cannot be hidden. Nor do men light a lamp, and put it under the peck-measure, but on the lamp stand; and it gives light to all who are in the house. Let your light so shine before men in such a way that they may see your good works, and glorify your Father who is in heaven."

➢ God wants to do an EXTREME MAKEOVER in your life. As you study His Word and are mentored by strong Christians who can walk through life with you, it will be like the process of being pregnant! At first when you surrender your life to God's will, you may or may not notice a significant difference. But, be assured as the days and months go by everyone will notice the difference and it will become very obvious that there have been some major changes in your life. They will want to know what has made this change.

➢ Even if you are not generally fond of rap ... meet Tamara Low and listen for a moment.

http://www.tangle.com/view_video?viewkey=c73f3c2bc263ad9e995a

I received this in an e-mail and found reference to it at:

http://beauty80.wordpress.com/2009/03/31/recall-notice-from-god

RECALL NOTICE

The Maker of all human beings, God, is recalling all units manufactured, regardless of make or year, due to a serious defect in the primary and central component of the heart. This is due to a malfunction in the original prototype unit's code named Adam and Eve, resulting in the reproduction of the same defect in all subsequent units.

This defect has been technically termed "Sub-sequential Internal Non-Morality," or more commonly known as S.I.N., as it is primarily expressed.

Some other symptoms include:

1. Loss of direction
2. Foul vocal emissions
3. Amnesia of origin

4. Lack of peace and joy
5. Selfish or violent behavior
6. Depression or confusion in the mental component
7. Fearfulness
8. Idolatry
9. Rebellion
10. Excessive Drinking

The Manufacturer, who is neither liable nor at fault for this defect, is providing factory-authorized repair and service free of charge to correct this SIN defect. The Repair Technician, Jesus, has most generously offered to bear the entire burden of the staggering cost of these repairs. There is no additional fee required.

The number to call for repair in all areas is: P-R-A-Y-E-R.

Once connected, please upload your burden of SIN through the REPENTANCE procedure. Next, download ATONEMENT from the Repair Technician, Jesus, into the heart component.

No matter how big or small the SIN defect is, Jesus will replace it with:

1. Love
2. Joy
3. Peace
4. Patience
5. Kindness
6. Goodness
7. Faithfulness
8. Gentleness
9. Self control

Please see the operating manual, the B.I.B.L.E. (Believers' Instructions Before Leaving Earth) for further details on the use of these fixes.

WARNING: Continuing to operate the human being unit without correction voids any manufacturer warranties, exposing the unit to dangers and problems too numerous to list and will result in the human unit being permanently impounded.

DANGER: The human being units not responding to this recall action will have to be scrapped in the furnace. The SIN defect will not be permitted to enter Heaven so as to prevent contamination of that facility.

Thank you for your attention.

GOD

Please assist where possible by notifying others of this important recall notice, and you may contact the Father any time by "kneemail."

In God We Trust

➤ If you don't know of a good church in your area, or you are looking for a mentor, you may wish to check out some of these resources. Look at their websites and call their offices to ask about good churches in your area. You may also listen to their radio programs, listen on-line to hundreds of programs and topics, some offer MP3, and podcasts. Check out their articles and get plugged in to people who can nurture you and help you grow:

- *Focus on the Family* – James Dobson – Broadcast in Washington, DC on WAVA 105.1 FM at 7:00 AM – Call this ministry at 800 / 232-6459 for other stations and times, or check out their website: *www.family.org*   I enjoy waking up to these helpful programs that give me wisdom for dealing with everyday situations.

- *Family Life Today* – Dennis Rainey (a ministry of Campus Crusade) – Broadcast in Washington, DC on WAVA 105.1 at 7:30 AM – Call this ministry at 800 / 358-6329 for other stations and times, or check out their website: *www.familylife.com* The Family Life Conference has ministered to many families on the edge of divorce. Lives have been changed and healing brings renewed love and devotion. Go to there website to find the conference closest to your area or go to a conference out of town and make this a gift to your spouse.

- *Truth for Life* - Alistair Begg offers great insights into God's word, is humorous, full of wisdom and grace as he tackles relevant topics. Listen live on his website: *www.truthforlife.org*

- *McLean Bible Church in McLean, VA* – Lon Solomon teaches God's word and calls people to accountability. Saturday night at 6:30 PM, Sunday morning at 9:00 AM, 10:45 AM, and 12:30 PM. Frontline is a wonderful ministry to 20 – 30 year olds that meets at 5:30 PM on Sunday's. Call 703 / 790-5590 for more information or visit *www.mcleanbible.org*. You may view these services live on your computer. Just open their website during the service times and join them on a live web cast. ... McLean Bible Church *www.mbclive.org* and *www.frontlinelive.com*

Also, check out this website for "*Not A Sermon Just A Thought*" by Lon Solomon, Pastor of McLean Bible Church in Northern Virginia: *www.notasermon.com*

- **Josh McDowell** Ministry exists to serve and to equip the Body of Christ in raising generations of purpose-driven Christians who know what they believe, ... *www.josh.org*

- **Ravi Zacharias** International Ministries (RZIM) - For 35 years **Ravi Zacharias** has spoken all over the world and in numerous universities, notably Harvard, Princeton, and Oxford University. ... To reach and challenge those that shape the ideas of culture with the credibility of the gospel of Jesus ... *www.rzim.org*

- Visit your local Christian Bookstores to ask about resources to help you grow, ask about good churches near where you live, and good books to read for areas where you struggle.

- Look in your local phone book or on the web for wonderful Christian ministries which can direct you to positive resources in your area:

  - ✓ Awana for young children
  - ✓ Young Life for teenagers
  - ✓ Youth for Christ
  - ✓ Campus Crusade for college age
  - ✓ Fellowship of Christian Athletes for all athletes – youth through college
  - ✓ Intervarsity Christian Fellowship for college age

❖ *Seven Tips for Prayerful Parents*

Many years ago on a soccer field, a friend said to me, "If there is one thing that you have done that I wish I had done for my son, it would be to get him involved in a church youth group." There is AWANA for little ones, Young Life for teenagers, Campus Crusade, Intervarsity, Fellowship of Christian Athletes and other church related Christian ministries. She noticed the choices my son was making and his strength of character in making decisions. She wished she had encouraged this type of input for her son.

It is really true that teenagers think their parents are old fashioned, square, and not in tune with today's society … therefore, to have someone who they can speak to, share with, bounce ideas off of that will give them solid, Christian advice and help them think through issues is a ***powerful resource*** that you want to have on your side! It is also very helpful, in particular as a single parent, to have the youth director to call upon when issues arise that they can address with your teenagers … without having you in the middle of the discussion. All it takes is a phone call to the youth director and asking him to address the issue … which he can do from a whole different reference point than I could as a parent. It works wonders and you will see results.

Your job is to make the phone call, then take your hands off of it and pray for their time

together. Be proactive! This is a wise plan of action which is freeing for both you and your teenager. Remember, an ounce of prevention is worth a pound of cure!!! Parents .... Know that you are empowered and not without hope! Take action!!! Fight for your kids!!!

This next resource is from "Family Life Today" a division of Campus Crusade for Christ, with a few modifications.

- Warning: Do not leave your children unprotected (un-prayed for). This makes them more susceptible to Satan's attack. The greatest shield of protection we as parents can provide for our children is prayer. Don't wait until you're desperate and left with "crisis praying." I Samuel 12:23, James 5:16, Colossians 4:2

- **<u>Specifics to Pray:</u>**

    1. I pray that God would place a protective hedge around our children so strong that Satan cannot enter and lead them into temptation. Psalm 33:20, James 5:8

    2. I pray that our children would use Godly wisdom in selecting their friends, for friends and peers do make a difference. Proverbs 1:10, Deuteronomy 13:6, 8. Ask God to give our children a discernment of people as well as knowing the difference between right and wrong, and pray that they choose to do what is right.

    3. I pray that our children would stay sexually pure in thought and in action. Psalm 24:4, Job 17:9

    4. I pray they will be caught if they wonder into cheating, lies or mischief. Proverbs 20:30

    5. I pray they will be alert and thinking clearly as they attend school and take exams. That they will be motivated to do the best they are capable of doing. Ephesians 4:2

6. I pray for my children and the husband / wife they one day will marry. Prepare them for each other even now. I pray that they will love the Lord with all their heart, soul and mind, and that they will be committed to a lifetime of marriage even when times get tough. I pray they will both have an appetite for spiritual truth, their goals and purposes will be the same and their future homes will be characterized by Deuteronomy 5:29 - "They will have such a heart in them, that they would fear Me, and keep all My commandments always."

7. I pray their lives will count for God and He will use them as a testimony and witness for His glory. I ask that they far exceed me in their spiritual lives. Psalm 103:17, 18, Isaiah 54:13, Psalm 78:1-8

We all know that *life is a battlefield and we have to learn how to fight for the heart and soul of our children or our spouse*, or the enemy will surely try to over take them. The key is beginning to realize that you don't have to reinvent the wheel. Draw upon other resources and people who have traveled these roads before, have answers and tools for your tool chest. Think outside your box and realize there is help available. Contact the resources listed above and get Godly wisdom on how to reach the heart and soul of your loved one. As a parent, your hands are not tied. **<u>Pick up your phone and take action for their wellbeing!</u>**

Here is an e-mail a father wrote in desperation to stop the chaos in their home. I have included comments in parenthesis as we worked through revisions to come up with something that would reach the heart and soul of this teenager and put him in touch with a counselor that could help them both work through their issues.

Taylor,

What happened last night was irrational, immature behavior on your part. There is no reason anyone should get as angry as you got and destroy everything in your path. (This may be very true – but she is wounded, angry, has had an abortion, life doesn't make sense at age 19 and you mentioned that you were screaming too… probably after she created a scene of destruction.)

When you come home we need to address these issues and decide together on principles and considerations on how we are going to live together with this issue and how you are going to get help to make sure that never happens again. I did nothing to deserve the yelling, screaming, and destruction you caused. (In the mind of a teenager whose parents are divorced, there is no security, there have been no secure family boundaries and warm fuzzies that say life will be okay when storms come. Steve and the world (TV, music, etc. have sold her a bag of goods that have only brought her mental baggage and bondage. She is running inside looking to find a safe place. She is lashing out because she has no more tools in her very limited tool box to fix her mom & dad. She doesn't know how to make the world a safe place to grow up in and probably doesn't have friends who are healthy, stable and secure.)

You are welcome to come home under these circumstances and I will be here to help you get better and support you through it. However it will take work and self control on your part to make this happen. (Very good … but we need to start with a clean slate where she knows the rules / principles for living and get them in writing and posted on her door. This all didn't get this way in a day and it will take time to clean up the mess and get this back on the right road. Prayerfully, the Sutherland's will intervene and work with both of you so that you can begin to hear one another and get to the heart of all the things that have brought you where you are today.)

Even though this behavior may have been given to you from your Mother, you need to change it before it is too late. No one succeeds being dishonest, manipulative or cruel and you need to learn that now before you destroy your life completely. (Ohhhhhh, a definite slap in the face to a child's mom or dad by the other parent never brings healing and security, but rather blame and deeper hurt. **You may feel that every word is true** … but if your goal is to look to find healing and more mature choices, there is a better way.)

This does not mean that I do not love you, quite the contrary; I love you very much and want the best for you. I know that you have many good qualities, are beautiful and can succeed (Very

Good ... no matter how hard this may have been to write or even if you don't fully believe it by her actions. God has only just begun and she has a long way to go. She needs hope, vision, purpose and direction.)

You need to step up and take action though and get on your right path. Not anyone else, but yours and I will be there to help and guide you. (Ken, ... What you say is very true ... but Taylor has no clue how to fix her world. She is confused and full of anger. Right now all she knows is brokenness. Rather than have her shut down emotionally and mentally, you want to draw her out and let her tell you where she hurts and begin to heal some of her hurts which will result in the actions you desire.)

I will not put up with that behavior again though. (Setting boundaries is good ... but first we need to put some "Principles for Living" in place. Then, and only then, when those principles are violated, the action is written as to what happens and there is no need for yelling.)

Dad

Here is the revised version that he actually sent:

Taylor,

I know you are hurting and probably feel like you have a huge hole in your heart. I know that I have one in mine. It is difficult to navigate life as a teenager and make any sense out of life and family when so many things appear to be upside down in your world. I know that I can't magically fix everything, but I would like the opportunity to work with you to rebuild a framework that provides a sense of security, family, guidelines that we both can live by, and lots of reasons for you to feel that I truly want God's best for you.

Love and respect are things that have gotten all turned around for us and I would like the opportunity to learn ways to communicate better, draw you out to know what's on your heart as we do the work to rebuild our lives together. Lashing out in destructive ways will only make things worse and will not solve anything. Instead of allowing these things to divide us and make things worse, my prayer is that you are willing to work with me to find solutions. Though we have both failed in the past, and there are ways that we both need to change to rebuild our lives, I will be here for you. It will take work and self-control for both of us.

Taylor, I love you very much and want the best things in life for you. I know that you have many wonderful qualities, are beautiful and have the ability to become all that God has for you. I would treasure the opportunity to get the help that we need and watch you blossom into the beautiful creation that God made you. You are a princess in His sight and in mine. As we put the right building blocks in place, you will have the opportunity to grow, mature and become even more beautiful than you can imagine.

I look forward to growing through life's situations with you.

With heartfelt love,
Daddy

❖ *Take Authority*

When the world is confusing and you can't find your way, don't forget in the darkness what you knew to be true in the light!

- Read God's Word, pray, wait to hear God's voice, and praise Him in the midst of the storm. Claim God's promises. He is able.

- Get around people who can lift you up and help you - A pastor, friend, parent.

- Tell others of your struggle - People can't help if you don't share your situation. Surrender your will and your pride today. They are keeping you in a self-made prison and only you have the key to unlock the door and give yourself permission to let yourself out.. Ask God for direction and an open door.

- Surrender your will and ask God for direction and an open door. You have an arsenal of help when you open up and contact resources that can offer you help and know how to fight the battle! Pick up your phone or go on-line and contact some of the resources mentioned today!

- Walk in authority, believing as you make your need known that a door will open.

- Run from the lies of this world.

- Watch what you read and see - Be careful not to fill your mind with trash! God gave you an eye gate and an ear gate ... you must filter what you let in!

- Expect great things from God ... Attempt great things for God! Check it out ... Luke 1:37, Luke 18:27, Titus 1:2

❖ *Website Resources*

➢ You won't have to look long to find that you do have resources at your fingertips and close to home.

➢ Websites for verse resources:

- *www.onesource.com*
- *www.biblegateway.com*
- *www.oneplace.com*
- *www.lightsource.com*

➢ *The Bible on One Page*: It's amazing to think of the work that went into putting this together. Be sure to scroll all the way to the bottom for an added blessing!

http://www.jrsbible.info/bible.htm

- *What Blood Type Are You?* I learned that a doctor's office may charge $30 to run a blood test ... or I could go to the Red Cross and offer to donate blood, and they will send you your blood type in a few weeks. So, being out of work, I decided to stop by the Red Cross, read through their information, speak with a consultant, and give a pint of blood, which I am told has the potential to save 3 lives!

- *Giving The Gift of Life*: Imagine, our bodies produce a substance like none other on earth. Which gives even greater meaning to the thought: The life is in the blood! And if we are willing to share it for the sake of another in need, about every 57 days or for round numbers every 60 days (2 months) we have the ability to help save the life of another, if not 3 others! I met people who come every 2 months or at least a couple times per year to give blood. Some because a relative was hospitalized and needed blood at one time and they wanted to give back to help another. Premiere donors, who came consistently, were calmly sitting there giving and using their laptop to keep up with the news of the day ... or whatever! If you've never taken the opportunity ... consider making an appointment to give the gift of life to another.

- *Give of Your Time and Talents*: When we give freely, often times we are the one who is blessed even more than the one whom we are serving! Have you ever sensed in your heart that you should help another, put it on your calendar and then other things started taking up your time and you really wanted to cancel your opportunity to serve? This happened to Leslie as she was sure God wanted her to help her long-time friend who lived in another city. When the weekend came for Leslie to be hands and feet for another, it would have been easy for her to cancel as too many other seemingly more important things had crowded into her schedule. She was taken back when Gail said, "Lighten up! You'll probably meet the man you will marry on the airplane!" It's an amazing story how it all came about, but Leslie's seat on the airplane turned out to be next to the man she is now engaged to marry! When you know in your heart that God calls you to serve, He may have a plan that is much broader than anything you imagined. Go willingly to bless another, serve with the gifts He has given you, and ultimately you will receive the blessing.

❖ *Wish List / Expenses / Savings / Giving*: Have you ever noticed that things you would like to have and feel you can't live without one month are not the same as the things you think you can't live without 2 months later? Think about it ... what did you get for Christmas last year, how about the year before and 3 years before that? What did you get for your birthday over the last 3 years? Isn't it amazing how quickly we forget! We are often like the kid in the candy store who thinks he/she must have the latest gadget and then it looses its appeal before long.

It is wise to place some boundaries / parameters around your spending if you want to stay free of debt. An easy method taught to kids is to have 4 envelopes.

1. <u>Giving</u> ... Right off the top ... or somehow there is never enough if you wait till the end!

2. <u>Saving</u> ... It's important to have something to draw upon on a rainy day when the car needs to be repaired, the roof leaks, or other unexpected expenses arise.

3. <u>Expenses</u> ... Housing, utilities, food, gasoline, etc.

4. <u>Spending</u> ... Otherwise called your "Wish List." And, may I suggest that you make a list of the items you "Wish for" and that you wait at least 24 hours before you make the purchase ... especially if it costs above a certain dollar amount. As you look at your "Wish List" from the previous week or month, how does this new "Wish" fit in priority wise with the other things on your list? If you are married, I suggest that you look at the list together and prioritize as to which item on the "Wish List" is purchased first to meet the needs of the family.

Another way to track your spending is to create a simple chart either on paper or on your computer with columns across the top of the page for date, vendor (store purchased from or the organization you gave to) giving, savings, housing / utilities, food, gasoline, kids sports, clothes, entertainment, etc., etc. Then you have a visual picture of where your hard earned dollars are going. Try it for a few months and you may be amazed at what you see when you look at the "big picture!"

❖ *Gain Interest and Grow Your Investment Without Loosing Your Principal! Learn about CD's and Annuities.* With our economy being so upside down, the stock market looking like a roller coaster ride, banks going under or being bought out, and the future insecure, do you know of a way to grow your investment, gain interest and not loose your principal (the money you initially invested)? Check out the information in the Appendix regarding CD's and Annuities to help you save, keep your principal, grow your investment and get the bonus! I have been extremely happy with my account growth during this down-turned market working with Rick Clark of Clark & Associates. His raspy voice is a sign that he is a cancer survivor! You can reach him or his seasoned office staff at 703 / 796-0957. You'll be glad you did!

❖ *Parents, Have You Reviewed Your Will Lately?* Do your grown children or grandchildren need your help now rather than later? One of my aunts in her 90's passed away a few years ago and it was discovered that she had put notes on things in her home that she would like given to various family members and grandchildren. The only problem is that many of them did not want the things she had picked out to give them, and the car she left to her grandchild sat idle for sooooooo long that it didn't work any more and wasn't needed by the time she died.

Would a better decision have been to ask her children and grandchildren what would be "meaningful to them" and help them in their time of need? Good food for serious thought. How can you minister to your family in ways that will be meaningful to them? Have you asked them lately? You may be surprised at their answers. They may have needs that they have not shared with you and you could bless them beyond measure if you only knew. Sharing your gift with them while you are alive allows you to receive the joy of knowing you were able to bless them.

Another very important consideration is the process you have used to decide who will be the executor of your will. If you haven't seen the DVD entitled **_The Ultimate Gift_**, I highly recommend it. It may give you some new insights, is delightful to watch, humorous and tells a great story that will warm your heart!
In years past, many times the oldest child was given this role as a birthright of some sort. However, history has shown that sometimes the wiser choice is to look at the heart and character of your children, family members or a trusted friend and determine who you think would most likely carry out your wishes.

❖ *Choose Your Battles:* I'm 20 and you need to let me make my own decisions. If you are a parent, you know there are a variety of things that can cause you to have or get grey hair! Having your 20 year old young adult (or any age for that matter) who basically tells you to "back off" and let them make their own decision on a matter can be a quick and interesting challenge of authority, particularly if it is a serious issue. It has often been said … "You have to choose your battles," and I truly believe that is an honest statement. Life if too short to deliberate them all and some things just are a matter of preference and not life and death choices, so give them some free reign.

We encountered these words from our pre-med student just before he was to head back to college for his 3rd year of study. He was on the college soccer team so they needed to report on the field by mid-August. The end of July and first few days of August, he decided to take the advice of someone who gave him a book they said would help him build more muscle mass if he ate just protein (meats) and fats (butter, bacon, etc.) for a week. Well, this proved to be disastrous for him! Choosing to strictly abide by this and a very low number of calories per day put his body is shock, and pulled down his immune system. Staying up to work on papers and computer items until 3 AM Sunday and Monday nights certainly didn't help his immune system. He was not feeling well on Monday, feverish on Tuesday and went home from work by 1:00 PM. Wednesday of that week he had a fever of 103.9 in the evening and thought he had a bad case of the flu. He did not want to take any aspirin, Tylenol, etc. but did accept cool clothes on his neck and forehead. His fever came down to 101 degrees. Thursday a friend who has studied homeopathy, Dr. Alyse Shockey, came over to speak with him and helped him with oils and breathing in hot steam with herbs to help loosen up the phlegm which caused him to cough up some of the junk in his lungs. Friday he felt some better, went for a morning walk, and then went back to bed because he felt dizzy. Friday night he told us he was 20 and we had to respect his wishes to get better without western medicine. He did not think he needed to see a doctor.

At this point I wish I had the wisdom to say ... "Here are your choices. You can get in the car and we will drive you to the Emergency Room, get some diagnostic tests to see what you actually have ... or ... we can call an ambulance to take you to the hospital and you can pay the bill for the ride! Either way, we are going and we are going NOW!"

Saturday morning his fever was still up and we knew we were headed for the Emergency Room where he did get a chest X-ray. The nurse assured him that he did have pneumonia and said you will take this antibiotic, as she handed him the pill and a cup of water. We all watched intently as he placed the antibiotic in his mouth and he swallowed. We breathed a sigh of relief! He was now on the road to recovery. He finally realized that when you have pneumonia, other serious illnesses, or any bacterial infections, your body needs an antibiotic to fight the germs to give your body what it needs to help you get well again!!! Don't listen to anyone who tells you otherwise as they are dangerous! I drove him back to his college campus, as he was too weak to drive any distance. I'm thankful to say he recovered nicely, however he missed the fall soccer season because he was too weak to practice or play. This was a hard lesson to learn. Whew!

❖ *Teach Another to Fish:* I was walking up to a store to run an errand and a young woman holding a 3 x 5 card approached me in the parking lot. The card read something like: "I am out of work and cannot pay my mortgage. I have 2 children and do not have formula for the baby. Would you kindly be willing to help?" Well, we all know that we can't feed the world ... but we can touch a life when God places someone in our path on a given day. I too am out of work and have been for 7 months, but I knew that my resources were more than whatever situation this young woman had. I don't know her full story, and I don't know if she knows who the baby's father is ... but I could provide formula for the baby. I asked about the baby's age and what formula she was feeding the baby.

We walked inside the store and saw that it was the most expensive brand. I showed her how to read the label of the store brand and compare the two. Actually there was a comparison right on the label of the store brand baby formula showing that the store brand had very close, if not more of some ingredients ... so ultimately it was not only half the cost, but better. I explained that often the same manufacturers use different labels on the same product. It is called marketing and she would need to learn to be wise to make her $ go further. I purchased two containers of the store brand formula for her. Instead of constantly giving a fish to another, teach them how to fish (compare labels in this case) so they can better fish for themselves in the future.

- ❖ *Shoes* ... I went looking for a pair of shoes, sensed I was supposed to go to a particular store and happened upon a 3-day sale! The shoes I liked were on the discontinued rack, happened to be my size, fit like a glove, and had already been discounted. This was my lucky day! Actually rather than coincidence, I believe it was God's intervention!

When I went up to the check-out counter, the lady rang up the shoes and they came up with a further discount. In addition, the store was offering a 15% discount, and all I had to do was sign up for a store card. If I did so, I would get the card in the mail, didn't have to use it (marketing ploy), and my balance would be a credit of $1.33. Mind you ... I hadn't paid anything for the shoes and she is offering me a credit of $1.33 if I signed up for a store card. So, being frugal and loving a bargain, I signed up for the store card and walked out of the store with the shoes in hand ... and a credit coming in the mail. Even if I never use the credit or the store card, you have to admit, I was astonished and you would have been too! If an occasional amazing gift walks up and presents itself to you ... take it and say Thank You! .... Oh, thought you might like to know that this occurred on the same day that I bought 2 containers of baby formula for the gal who needed food for her baby!

❖ *Questions to Ask Before You Marry! … See Attachment in Appendix …* I'm sure you would agree that having the presence of mind to think with your head and not only with your heart is invaluable! When you take two imperfect people and put them together in a relationship where their vows state that they are committed to love and cherish one another for a lifetime, it would be wise to go in with a little knowledge. It is common knowledge that even the best of marriages have their struggles, as does any relationship with someone that you truly care about. Sooooooo, do yourself a favor and don't be afraid to find out how this wonderful person you are dating and considering marrying thinks on a variety of topics! You may be surprised … but better to find out now rather than after you tie the knot on your wedding day!

❖ *Where Are You Looking?* … Some of us are at the airport of convenience (instant gratification) when we should be at the dock of obedience where we will find God's blessing! If your boyfriend wants to shack up, tell him it will cost him a lifelong commitment and a ring. Real Men respect what they pay for! Chuck Swindol, on his radio program entitled Insight for Living **www.insightforliving.com** reminds us that playing house and sleeping around will constantly produce a "gallery of images on the canvas of your mind." Know that God provided you with the right parts. There is No Need to give it a variety of test runs! Satan laughs every time we fall for the lie that we should try it our way and give in to lust instead of the commitment of marriage. God calls us to renew our minds. See Romans 12:1-2 and Ephesians 5 and 6. Besides, have you ever thought about the fact that if someone will sleep around before marriage, this habit may be very hard to break after marriage!

Therefore, since we have so great a cloud of witnesses surrounding us, let us also lay aside every encumbrance, and the sin which so easily entangles us, and let us run with endurance the race that is set before us, fixing our eyes on Jesus, the author and perfecter of faith, who for the joy set before Him endured the cross, despising the shame, and has sat down at the right hand of the throne of God. Hebrews 12:1-2

For the word of God is living and active and sharper than any two-edged sword, and piercing as far as the divisions of soul and spirit, of both joints and marrow, and able to judge the thoughts and intentions of the heart. And there is no creature hidden from His sight, but all things are open and laid bare to the eyes of Him with whom we have to do. ……He has been tempted in all things as we are, yet without sin. Let us therefore draw near with confidence to the throne of grace, that we may receive mercy and may find grace to help in time of need. Hebrews 4:12-16

This is an excerpt from **Our Daily Bread**, August 15, 2010 … God is our refuge and strength, a very present help in trouble … entitled "Mightier Than All" Psalm 23. Iguazu Falls on the border of Brazil and Argentina is a spectacular waterfall system of 275 falls along 2.7 km (1.67 miles) of the Iguazu River. Etched on a wall on the Brazilian side of the Falls are the words of Psalm 93:4, "Mightier than the thunders of many waters, mightier than the waves of the sea, the Lord on high is mighty!" (RSV). Below it are these words, "God is always greater than all of our troubles."

The writer of Psalm 93, who penned its words during the time that kings reigned, knew that God is the ultimate King over all. "The Lord reigns," he wrote. "Your throne is established from of old; You are from everlasting" (vv.1-2). No matter how high the flood or waves, the Lord remains greater than them all.

The roar of a waterfall is truly majestic, but it is quite a different matter to be in the water hurtling toward the falls. That may be the situation you are in today. Physial, financial, or relational problems loom ever larger and you feel like you are about to go over the falls. In such situations the Christian has Someone to turn to. He is the Lord, "who is able to do exceedingly abundantly above all that we ask or think" (Ephesians 3:20) for He is greater than all of our troubles. – C. P. Hia

If you are helpless in life's fray,
God's mighty power will be your stay;
Your failing strength He will renew,
For He's a God who cares for you. – D. De Haan

Never measure God's unlimited power by your limited expectations.

Chapter 10

✓ **Lots of "General Tips" you may find helpful!**

A potpourri of topics to tickle your funny bone and help you "think outside the box!"

❖ How much do you pay for the *ink cartridges for your printer*? Would you like to pay less? Consider checking out the following link and others like it to *get drastically reduced rates on your ink cartridges.* You order them on-line, they come to you in a day or two in the mail. You save money on gas and time driving to the store to pick them up. You return them in a plastic postage paid mailer and get credit towards your next purchase! Now that's a Great Idea!!! I pay anywhere from $9.00 to $11.49 per black ink cartridge for my Dell printer and smile that I am no longer paying $25 to $35 per cartridge that I used to buy from the local store! Check it out: *www.enviroinks.com*

❖ Occasionally it pays to stop in a store you haven't been in for a while. I did this recently and learned that Walgreens will *refill your empty ink cartridges* for your printer during their sale week for $9.99 ... Now that's a Great Idea!!! If it's not a sale week, it may cost you $12.99, which is still a huge savings over the cost of a new purchase. I also discovered that my local postal service store at the shopping center offers this same service and gives discounts! Check it out. You'll be glad you did!

- *Have you discovered:* <u>www.freecycle.org</u> ... The Freecycle Network™ is made up of 4,810 groups with 7,245,000 members across the globe. It's a grassroots and entirely nonprofit movement of people who are giving (& getting) stuff for *FREE* in their own towns. It's all about reuse and keeping good stuff out of landfills. Each local group is moderated by a local volunteer (them's good people). Membership is free. To sign up, find your community by entering it into the search box or by clicking on "Browse Groups" above the search box. Have fun! ... Free Cycle ... Changing the world one gift at a time!

- If someone is trying to sleep in a dorm room or at home near where you are typing at the keyboard, consider purchasing a *"Quiet Keyboard."* With Quite-Type Key Technology. I've seen them for $6.00 at Big Lots. They really do make a difference!

- If you are painting and need to stop, but don't want to clean out the **paint brush** yet and loose all that paint that is stored up in the bristles, *simply wrap your paint brush in SaranWrap and it will stay nice and moist* for a day or so till you can get back to painting! Obviously, when you finish painting you will want to clean out your brush real good.

- **Whitelight Tooth Whitening System** whitens teeth FAST using Light Technology. I bought this kit in a local store a few years ago and it truly works quickly. It came with a gel to put in a dental tray that sits on your teeth, and a light that fits comfortably right next to your teeth. The specially formulated gel rapidly removes surface stains and penetrates deep to remove embedded stains. It works great on stains caused by coffee, tea, smoking, red wine, fruit juice, aging, and more. White Light uses the same active ingredient used by dentists so there is no harm to your teeth. Check it out at *www.10minteethwhitening.com* and I hope you are as pleased as I have been! The light stays on for 10 minutes and does an awesome job of whitening. If you have persistent stains, it is fine to push the button for another 10 minutes and check your results! I can no longer find this product in the store locally for refills of the specially formulated gel, but have ordered it recently on-line and it was shipped to me.

- Did you know! *Teeth* … Yes, teeth! Until recently I never realized that if you happen to have a tooth that is taller than your others … *your dentist very easily can file it down to match your other teeth!* Miracle of miracles! Now you would have thought they would have told you this years ago! Duh! It's like filing down your finger nail and there is NO Pain!!! Now, why didn't all the dentists over the years tell us it was that easy???

- *Green Vibrance* is a wonderful product that you can get from your local health food store. If they don't carry it, you can reach them at: 1 / 800 – 242-1835 or <u>www.vibranthealth.us</u> or <u>mail@vibranthealth.us</u> . It gives me tons of energy and has 25 Billion Probiotics Per Dose from 12 Strains. *It is a restorative, concentrated Superfood in powder form.* I like to mix cran-raspberry juice with either mango or orange juice each morning and then add a scoop full of Green Vibrance to start my day, followed by a bowl of cereal with Craisins, a mixture of walnuts, almonds and pecans, a banana, blueberries, strawberries and milk of course! Yum!

- *Calcium* … We all know that as we get older our doctors tell us we need to take calcium to keep our bones strong. Well, I tried taking calcium and got cramps in my feet. So I stopped taking it. Then I learned that there are different kinds of calcium and they react differently in the body. Calcium Carbonate is like eating crushed up seashells … not good. *Calcium Citrate is highly absorbable* and when mixed with Magnesium, Zinc and D it is even better for you! … And I don't get cramps in my feet, toes and legs any more!

- Heat up *leftover pizza* in a nonstick skillet on top of the stove. Set heat to med-low and heat till warm. This keeps the crust crispy. No soggy micro pizza. A cooking channel recommended this and it really works.

- Have you ever looked for a quality program that will enhance the lives of your kids and bring a blessing to you at the same time? Have they ever been mountain biking, horseback riding, had breakfast on the range, gone parasailing, away to the mountains or a huge lake with about 300 other kids where they had the time of their lives away from electronic gear for a whole week? If not, do them and yourself, and the whole family a favor and check out the *Young Life (YL)* website as they have over 30 years of experience in knowing how to reach the heart of your teenager. They will have the time of their lives and the food is really awesome … really! ☺ *Young Life* may even have a presence in your local high school on a weekly basis, and summer opens the door to more than 22 camps across the US and abroad. Check it out and you'll be glad you did … and so will they! For junior high there is *Wyldlife,* and *Young Life* does an awesome job working with and ministering to your senior high students. *Capernaum* is their ministry to kids and young adults with disabilities. More information can be found at your local Young Life office or at *www.younglife.org* They also have lodging for adults to visit their camps for a week so you can be "a fly on the wall" while 300 kids have a week they will remember for a lifetime! Call today to make your reservation!

- If you're getting older and your eyes have trouble seeing an account number or phone number on a page, color the item with a *yellow highlighter* and it will stand out and be much easier to read!

- *Getting ticks off yourself and your dog* … Have you ever thought of using a hair blower??? It works like a charm! Just turn the hair blower on warm and wave it slowly, about 6 inches above where the tick has planted itself on your dog … or on you! Be careful not to burn yourself or your dog. **The tick will not like the heat and will pull its head out and fall on the floor.** Use a tissue to wrap it in and flush it down the toilet. Make sure to follow-up with an antiseptic at the spot where the tick was on you or your dog! If you notice anything unusual over the next few days or weeks, or if your dog won't eat treats, drags a leg, or is throwing up, get some blood work done and check for lime disease before it spreads to the liver. If tests show positive for lime, get an antibiotic quickly.

- Have you ever been *driving* and realized that you were just tooooooo tired to continue and needed to *rest*. Sometimes coffee is not what you need. Sometimes it's a short nap that will revitalize your system and then some coffee to wake up your rested body! Sometimes I have stopped for a few minutes at a church parking lot, gas station or shopping mall. Other times, I start looking at the exit signs for those with hotels and motels. On one very warm summer day where it was way too hot out to sit and rest in my car with the doors locked, I pulled off an exit that had 3 hotels/motels. I just needed a place to sit in some air conditioning and close my eyes for 15 minutes or a ½ hour. It felt soooooo good to rest my eyes and be still. *A 20 minute cat-nap can do you wonders and then you are refreshed and ready to go again!* Once you are rested, stop and get a cup of coffee or a bite to eat and then you're on your way, rested, refreshed and ready to go!

❖ If you are a real people person and are drained by working on *paperwork at home alone*, *pack up your papers and head for places where people are*, like your local library, a bookstore that has chairs or tables where you can work, a large fast-food restaurant, a nice hotel lobby, a park, a coffee shop like Starbucks, Panera Bread, a fountain or town center.

❖ Do you ever have those wonderful brainstorms or remember there is something else you want to get at the grocery store and think you won't forget only to realize a few minutes later that it has completely gone out of your conscious thinking! Oh, if you had only written it down. Sometimes I even wake up in the middle of the night and my brain starts rolling with ideas or something I need to recall. I have tried making an acrostic out of the beginning letters of the words I want to remember to help me recall the word when I wake up. This works some of the time, but I find it more reliable to *keep a small flashlight, paper and pencil near my pillow,* or between the two pillows, so I can jot down a word or two and then drift back to sleep. If you're like me, you need to print in big letters or else you can't read it in the morning! I now need a pair of glasses to go with the paper, flashlight and pencil!

❖ It also helps to keep *paper and a pencil or pen* in the car, in your purse or briefcase, etc. *Writing a quick note saves a lot of time trying to remember that important item you didn't want to forget!* Keeping post-it notes in the car works great as you can attach them to your dash or your notebook or your purse … so you remember what you needed to do! And … don't forget to keep a flashlight in your car. It may just come in handy!

- You can *hang around a garage all day and it doesn't make you a car*! The same is true at church. You can attend many services and talk to a lot of people, but it doesn't make you a Christian. The Bible says: "For God so loved the world that he gave His only begotten son that whosoever (that's you and me) believeth in Him shall have everlasting life." (John 3:16) Think about it ... I am a love stain of Jesus because He died for me.

- The miracle of a conversion happens in a moment ... the miracle of a saint happens in a lifetime! *God has given us instructions on how to live* ... now if we will only listen and obey. Have you taken time to communicate with God today? He created you and knows the plans He has for you today. If you are not in a Bible study, you may want to learn about His perspective on your life, your thoughts, your actions, and your heart's condition toward Him.

- *Gardening Tip* ... Start putting in your plants, work the nutrients of Miracle Grow into your soil. Wet newspapers and layer them around the plants overlapping as you go, cover with mulch and forget about weeds. Weeds will get through some gardening plastic; however, they will not get through wet newspapers.

- Have you ever eaten something that had *something really hot* in it (like jalapeno peppers) and your mouth and throat were on fire??? Well I have, and one time I drank every pitcher of cream for coffee that was on the big round table, and someone suggested that I put butter on bread and that would coat my throat to ease the burning. However, I since learned that *opening a packet of sugar* (which you can find on most any table) and pouring some in your mouth will calm the burning almost immediately. Somehow there is a chemical reaction and I am thankful to have learned about this one!

- *If you are one who takes off your ring(s)* when you wash your hands in a public restroom, *first put a white paper towel on the countertop and place your ring(s) on the paper towel*, then wash your hands. Use another paper towel to dry your hands. You will still see your ring(s) sitting on the counter top on the white paper towel and not forget to put them back on your finger(s) before leaving!

CHAPTER 10 ▪ 111

Way too many people have forgotten rings in restrooms and never seen them again.

❖ Even though I now wear contacts or glasses, something that seems difficult is threading a hand sewing needle or the sewing machine needle. If you have had this same experience, there is hope! Recently I learned that G Street Fabrics (and I'm sure other sewing stores have them as well), carries ***"self-threading sewing needles!"*** Now that's a Great Idea! You simply slide the thread down the side of the needle and it slips into a tiny slot and threads the needle!!! I like it. I really like it!!! They call them handicap needles … and I would like to suggest that they change the name to "Self-Threading Sewing Needles." Anyway, I sure bought some!

❖ Probably the most time consuming thing about <u>***making lasagna***</u> is that I was taught to cook the noodles, cook the meat, and then layer these with the cottage cheese and mozzarella. After experimenting, I learned that briefly cooking the lasagna noodles is helpful but only for a few minutes so they are easier to work with and bend a little. Adding a tsp of oil to the water keeps them from sticking together. (It also works to use the noodles right out of the box.) Then mix the uncooked meat (low fat) with the cottage cheese, spaghetti sauce, spices and some mozzarella cheese and layer this mixture together between the noodles. Top with some additional sauce, mozzarella cheese and spices. It all cooks together and the noodles absorb the flavors and the moisture. Yum!

❖ *Hiccups!* Have you found a good way to get rid of them quickly that works every time??? Well, try this. Fill a small cup about ½ full. Bend forward, almost in half, take a small sip from the far side of the cup and swallow. Take another small sip and swallow. Do it a 3rd time. Now, slowly stand up and smile. Your hiccups are gone! It has something to do with the air and water passing down your throat, but it works every time!

❖ *Vacation housing or renting a house for an out of town wedding.* My sister, Sue, and her husband, Ned, have done this on a variety of occasions and it has been delightful. When you have a large group of people coming from out of town for a wedding, graduation or family reunion, why rent a ton of hotel rooms when you can enjoy a large living room together, a sunroom, or waterfront property. In a home setting, you can enjoy your family with much more interaction than you would have by staying at a hotel. They often rent the house for the week prior to the wedding, invite the other parents and their family members to stay so they can get to know one another better. This also brings people together in helping and feeling included in the festivities prior to the event. These are some websites you may find helpful:

www.vbro.com   *www.homeaway.com*
www.a1vacations.com   *www.homeexchange.com*

- ❖ *Did you bring the camera?* Have you ever asked that question and wished you had remembered so that you could *capture that "Kodak Moment!"* Well, now you can. Simply purchase a throw away type camera at most any grocery or convenience store and keep it in the glove compartment of your car or in your purse. Also, it comes in handy if you have an accident and you can take pictures of the scene and damages!

- ❖ I always carry a small digital camera with me as you just never know when that Kodak moment will occur! When I have a lot of *pictures to print*, I like to stand at the kiosk at my local Target and size them, print them, and hold them in my hand almost immediately. Doing it this way, I pay 19 to 29 cents per print. However, I am learning that I can save a lot of money if I would sit at home and go to Snapfish, choose my pictures to print, send them to Walgreens or Costco and pay 9 cents per print!!! Now that's a Great Idea!

- ❖ If you have ever experienced *pain in the metatarsal area of your foot* (just below the toes), you know that it can be extremely painful. Correct-A-Step Orthotics has done wonders for my feet and the pain is gone. Putting these supports in your shoes redistributes your body weight and takes the pressure off of the metatarsal area, thus relieving the pain. Contact Norval & Edith Pennington, O.T., C.O.S., Ped at 256 / 586-4817 or check their website at *www.correct-a-step.com* for more information.

- It used to be that when I had some work done here at the house that I would file away the papers in my tax box for that year, and then the next time I needed to remember the name of the contractor for another job, I had to go digging for the information. Since then *I have started a spreadsheet on the computer with date of service, name of contractor, contact info, list of repairs made, and comments*. It saves a lot of time and I know to look in the "Home Repairs" file.

- If you're anything like me, variety is the spice of life and it is nice to have a variety of earrings, necklaces and bracelets with you when you travel to match your outfits. Upon arriving at my destination I often discovered that all the necklaces had somehow become entangled with other necklaces and earrings and I had to sort out my collection by dumping them all out of my pull string pouch. One day upon return home and going through some sewing items I came across a shoulder pad in my sewing drawer and it occurred to me that this may be just the ticket to resolve the jumble. *I pushed the posts of the earrings through the shoulder pad and nicely organized my earrings.* Why didn't I think of this before? Then I put the shoulder pad into a see-through fabric bag with pull string (purchased from the craft store) and my earrings were all conveniently organized and ready. I purchased some small zip-lock bags from the craft store and put matching necklaces and earrings in those. Ahhhhhh, no more tangles!

- *No more mosquitoes* … Place a dryer sheet in your pocket and in your socks. It will keep the mosquitoes away.

- *Planning ahead.* Have you ever wished you had thought ahead and placed a few items in your car so you can switch gears and do things with friends without driving all the way home? It could be as simple as *keeping some of the following items in your car* …assuming you drive most places: walking shoes, a pair of shorts or slacks, a change of clothes, a light jacket, a blanket for a picnic, a small lawn chair. How about a few emergency kit items: triple antibiotic and band aids, ace bandage, scissors, bottle of water, paper towels, tissues, and a flashlight. Duck tape and a few bungee cords fix lots of things!!!

- **Suitcase & Travel** .... Have you ever noticed when you travel that they don't always put wall plugs where you can easily reach them? Toss an adaptor that holds 3 plugs and an extension cord in your suitcase to resolve these issues. Don't forget to take along a flashlight too so you don't wake others in the middle of the night or if you are looking for your jogging clothes early in the morning. Ah, and a night light in the bathroom keeps you from needing to turn on that big bright light and waking yourself up at 3 in the morning when you walk into the bathroom.

- Have you ever heard of **an adult who has the symptoms of diaper rash** where the skin is red and irritated? Some treat this with steroid crèmes which may help temporarily. If this does not work long term, it may be a fungus. Try treating it for 3 days with Fluconazole Tablets 150 mg by mouth. Mix triple antibiotic ointment and Nystatin 100,000 which is an antifungal yellow crème medication in your hand and apply to red irritated skin. If it is a fungal infection, you should see results in 3 days. If it is not completely gone, you may have to repeat tablets and crème for another 3 days. This should clear it up completely. What a blessing!

- Do you need to track your blood pressure on a daily or weekly basis and wish there was an easier way than the arm cuff? **Dr. Leonard's wrist blood pressure monitor** is accurate and very easy to use … and easy for travel. For more information on this product and other medical products go to *www.drleonards.com* or call 800 / 785-0880.

http://www.drleonards.com/Health-Products/Blood-Pressure-Monitors/Wristech-Blood-Pressure-Monitor/99293.cfm?clicksource=HOME_PAGE_IMAGE

Wrist Blood Pressure Monitor … Discount Coupon Code: **ULTCPD**

Coupons: *http://www.ultimatecoupons.com/cp/11112/38517.htm*
A friend told me about this and uses it every day. He checked with his doctor and it is accurate and very easy to use.

Other things to know about blood pressure … Lemonade, oranges and garlic have been shown to reduce blood pressure. Oranges are high in potassium which helps to regulate your blood pressure. If you are deficient in potassium, you will have high blood pressure. Do some research and enjoy the benefits of lower blood pressure. Also, Bruce has been drinking the mangosteen juice daily and his personal testimony is that he no longer needs his blood pressure meds as his blood pressure has come into normal range. Check with your doctor after drinking Xango's Mangosteen Juice to see if you get the same results!

- Have you ever wished you could find a source of "Solutions to Everyday Product Problems, Support, Manuals, Troubleshooting and Product Recommendations?" **FixYa** offers an online tech support community where experts and consumers meet to solve their appliance and gadgets technical problems. They offer comprehensive repair and troubleshooting solutions for absolutely everything you can think of 24/7. Go to *www.fixya.com* for a 7-Day Free Trial. Just "remember to cancel anytime during your 7 day trial" if you don't want to keep this service or you will be charged $9.99 for your monthly subscription.

- Do you or your children ever have *sleepless nights or hear voices that are troubling*? I encouraged a friend to pray and ask the Lord to take the voices away ... and here is his response...

Sharon had been complaining today about hearing the voices and at one time started to cry because they were scaring her. Sharon and I went to Best Buy and got a radio for her room. Tonight she got into bed, I knelt beside the bed and out loud prayed that Jesus would protect her and take the voices away and out of her head. I asked Jesus to kick them out of her head and her room, and not let them come back in.

Now normally it will take her about an hour or more to go to sleep and sometimes she would even get up scared with the voices. However, after praying, Sharon was asleep in 5 minutes and that was about two hours ago. Praise the Lord. Tomorrow when she gets up we'll both pray together that she is protected all day from the voices. ... A day later he wrote back: Thank you again. Both nights Sharon and I prayed, turned the radio on to Christian music and she was asleep in 5 minutes. David

- If you are ever still awake at the wee hours of the morning and **need to get good sleep to wake up refreshed in the morning**, check with your pharmacist or doctor for a solution. The health food store even has products to help you relax and get a good night's sleep. I have discovered I can be asleep in minutes with the smallest amount of Ambien 5 mg. The pills are already really small, but I place a few pills in wax paper or saran wrap and hit them lightly with a hammer to crush them and put the pieces back in the bottle. On occasion when I can't seem to go to sleep, I take the smallest little piece with some water and within minutes I am gone to the world and wake up refreshed. Every person is different, so try it on a day off and see how your body responds. Here's to a "Refreshing Good Night's Sleep!" Natural products like Melatonin may work well for you, so please check with your local health food store and your doctor.

- In the fast-paced stressful world that we live in, **many people experience long-term depression**. If you let it go untreated, you may face a downward spiral that you can't seem to get out of that will affect you and those you love for a lifetime! Please seek help to deal with the issues and gain a new perspective in speaking with others who have walked in your shoes. Learn about the tools to rebuild relationships or resolve issues so you can begin to see the light of hope at the end of the tunnel and walk into the sunshine of new tomorrows. It's always too soon to quit! There are answers. There is help, hope and purpose. Growth, working to understand another's point of view and change may be your best friend. Talk to your doctor, your pastor, a friend, a counselor, read some of the books suggested in these chapters, and watch a DVD on communication. You'll be glad you did!

- If someone you know is an alcoholic, set up a tape recorder or your camera to video them on a couple of different occasions. When they are sober, invite those who love them over and **tell the alcoholic you have something you want them to see**. They probably won't believe they actually "act out like that" when they are drunk. Seeing themselves in action may be what it takes for them to realize that they need to get help NOW! You may also write them a letter assuring them of your love and desire to see them get well for the good of the family. Do the research for them, pack some of their clothes and have a car ready to take them while they are not in denial of what they just saw.

Here's a note from my dear friend, Melissa: *We were tough. We gave Ross little "wiggle" room and we were very, very tough. I am happy to share the letters that we wrote if they would help. It was extremely difficult to do, but I felt that we were saving our son, so it was worth it. I never have to say that I did not do all that I could do. We drove Ross to Penfield Christian Homes in Georgia where he stayed for a couple months. It is for adult men and the cost was around $2,500 which is very reasonable! I do not know if there is one for young women but we can sure find out. The thing that I am learning is that there are so many young people who are struggling with the same issues. It is amazing how many friends I have shared this with in the past few weeks that have members of their families going through, or who have gone through the same thing. It is sad. Perhaps though we can all help each other.*

Ross now has his driver's license again, has been accepted for a job he is very excited about, has a new attitude about life and looks like a different person with vision, hope, determination and purpose. Getting him the right kind of help truly has resulted in a major transformation in his life! What a blessing!!! Love, Melissa

❖ *You and Your Metabolism!* Have you ever noticed when you are stuck in traffic or even at home between meal time that you are hungry. Possibly it shows up as feeling out of sorts or just not at your peak. Try putting a jar of Trail Mix in your car or having it available in your office desk, or at home in the kitchen. You will be amazed at what a few handfuls of protein can do for you at about 10:30 AM and at about 4:00 PM when you feel the lull and need a pick-me-up. I even keep a snack size zip-lock bag of trail mix in my purse for a quick "refueling" of my energy! The Trail Mix I like best is a Safeway brand or the Mountain Trail Mix from Walmart. They both have peanuts, almonds, raisins and a few small chocolate pieces. I add walnuts and pecans. Yum!!!

❖ *Are you looking for a group of people who have your same interests?* Try looking at this website: www.meetup.com Type in your zip code and the activity you are looking for whether it is book clubs, skiing, sailing, tennis, or hiking and see what is in your area. Your new friends may be closer than you think.

- *Events & Adventures* – A fun way to meet other singles. Call them at 800 / 386-0866. This may open the door to cultural outings, sporting events, wine tasting, kayaking, volleyball, comedy night, jet skiing, billiards, horseback riding, etc. *http://www.eventsandadventures.com/thanks.html*

- *Yams and potatoes* grow spuds if left unattended for a while. If you would like a lovely green plant, slice off a piece of the yams or potatoes with the spud and sit them in a shallow container with water. Before long you will see the greenery appear. It will grow into a *lovely green plant* and become a great conversation piece in your kitchen!

- Working at a *Farmer's Market* can be a fun adventure and you just may come home with a basket of goodies as a thank you from the vendors. Deb discovered the vendors do not want to haul items back to the farm and they will appreciate your willingness to be there at 6:30 AM to help them set up their stands and work with them until noon. It's a great way to meet new people, help the vendor, customers and you will certainly save on your grocery bill for the week!

- There are some awesome **Christian T-shirts** available at the Heavenly T-shirts website *www.heavenlyt-shirts.com* about Prayer, Jesus, Bible, Cross Tees and more. Also check out *www.heavenlyt-shirts.com/freestuff* for FREE STUFF.

- Do you remember when the telephone company didn't charge to give you a phone number? Now they charge $1.00 to $1.50 to get a phone number from information. *Google has a FREE service* that is great when you are driving or on the road with no pen, pencil or paper handy. Don't waste your money on *information calls* and don't waste your time manually dialing the number. Here's a number worth putting in your cell phone, or your home phone speed dial: 1-800-goog411

If you are driving along in your car and need to call the golf course and don't know the number, hit the speed dial (that you have programmed) for Information. This is a nationwide service and it is absolutely free!

The voice at the other end says, "City & State." I say, "Garland, Texas ." He says, "Business, Name or Type of Service." I say, "Firewheel Golf Course." He says, "Connecting" and Firewheel answers the phone. How great is that?

Click on the link below and watch the short video clip for a quick demonstration: **http://www.google.com/goog411**

❖ *Getting a tan*. Ah yes, I love those warm summer days at the beach and truly enjoy smelling like a coconut while I'm getting my tan! ***The trick is figuring out how to get a gorgeous tan without burning.*** I don't know if this will work for you, but it seems to work like a charm for me. The first couple of times I spend some time in the sun, and park my body on the beach or in the yard or by the pool, I want to really protect my skin, so I start with 30 SPF (which blocks the UV rays) and then apply my favorite oil. If it smells like Hawaii and the tropics I like it all the better. When I close my eyes I can smell the coconut scent and pretend I see the palm trees swaying! Mentally I'm a world away enjoying the warmth of the summer sun. After an hour or so, I make sure to check to see that my plan is working and press on my arm and leg to see if there is any sign of tanning, which is usually the case. Then as the season moves more into summer and I spend a little more time in the sun, I switch to SPF 15 and oil and continue to enjoy a beautiful tan without any sign of burning. The key is to limit your time in the sun and find a way to stop the bad rays and absorb the good ones! Be wise ... and don't stay out in the sun all day!

❖ If you have trouble *applying suntan lotion to your back*, take along a long wooden spoon type utensil with a nice long handle. I purchased mine in a bag of 3 at the dollar store. They are made of ***white plastic*** and work great!!! I keep one in my beach bag, one on my dresser for applying cream on my back after a shower, and I keep one in my suitcase for when I travel! Apply lotion to the ***long spoon utensil*** which makes it easy to apply it to your back! It also makes a great back scratcher. Of course, if you have someone who can apply lotion or scratch your back for you, that's very nice!

❖ ***Beach Blanket.*** Have you ever seen families with their bedroom quilt, wool blanket or a blanket from the room they are renting as they trudge with all their stuff toward the beach? Well, why not just **take an old sheet along with you as your "beach blanket."** It is very lightweight, easy to carry, fits in your carry-all bag, is very easy to wash and dry quickly for your next trip to the beach! Also, it's not hot to lay on in the warm summer sun!

❖ Save your ***old toothbrushes*** as they are great for using with soap to clean spots off of cloths, cleaning the bottom of tennis shoes, cleaning around fixtures or in tiny grooves and hard to reach places.

❖ In the craziness of life, sometimes it good to stop and ***look in the mirror*** to see what needs fixing. Look from the front and then take a look from the side. Remember, how you see yourself and how another sees you can be two very different views! I recently met a lovely lady named Robin who had the same hairdo for years and years. We so easily become accustomed to doing things the same way that sometimes it takes encouragement to consider changing. Well, I'll let you decide, but here are the before and after photos. ***A new style, some color and highlights*** make her look at least 10 to 15 years younger! What a transformation!!! It does wonders for the self-image. She loves it and has received sooooooo many compliments. Now that's a Great Idea!!! Hugs to you! Now it's your turn to take a look in your mirror!

- Have you ever wanted to *"try-on" someone else's hair style* to see if it would look good on you? Well, now you can. Go to <u>www.instyle.com</u> and you can up-load your photo, choose your face shape and try on hair styles of Hollywood stars! It's a fun website and its FREE, so have fun, laugh a lot and see what looks best on you. You can even choose your hair color! I also visited Bravado Wigs (**10415 North St., Fairfax, VA 22030 ... 703 / 352-4247**) to try on all styles of wigs to see what looked best! It's good to laugh at yourself, get some new ideas, and see "the new you!" Just maybe ... there is a much better style for you!

- *Wilsire Wigs!* I was in the checkout line at the grocery store and complimented the checker on her hair style. She looked at me, smiled and said you can have a hairdo like this too! She said that wigs are very popular in New York and California and the way they make them today is much nicer than the older types. These breath, have blended colors to look more natural and are very comfortable. She suggested that I check out the *Wilshire Wigs website* as they have a huge number of styles and colors. She said she works two jobs and doesn't have time to bother with her hair. What a time saver! *www.wilshirewigs.com*

- Whether you are planning on traveling and looking for *clothing that you don't have to worry about wrinkling*, or just like the fun of having something different that looks great, check out some fun choices with great color combinations by visiting the Magic Scarf website ... *www.magicscarf.com* and you'll be amazed at some fun items to choose from. I especially like the origami two color blouses.

- Remember the song .... *Don't Save It All For Christmas Day (Avalon)* ... Remember ... Everyday can be Christmas ... It's all about a spirit of giving, joy and encouraging one another! Encourage someone today and it will put a smile on their face and a song in your heart!

- Have you ever looked at a number on caller ID or on a piece of paper and wondered whose number it might be? Well check this out. Go to: *www.address.com* and then click on *Reverse Look Up*. For FREE it will give you the person's name, address and phone number.

- *Real Estate Tip: People like to buy a home that "feels like home."* Heat up some cookies for 5-7 seconds in the microwave and the aroma makes it feel like home! Yummy ... just like right out of the oven!

- *Think outside the box!* Do you ever come to a "mental dead-end" when trying to figure something out and just don't see another way to get it accomplished ... then it's time to *"think outside the box!"* Talk with friends; think about how someone else might solve this. Check the website entitled *www.askjeeves.com* , or Google it! When it comes to "Mr. Fix It" projects, I think, okay, how would my dad resolve this? Thankfully, sometimes it gets my mental wheels turning and I think of alternative ways to tackle the issue.

- ❖ Ah yes, my *hot water bottle*! Have you ever had one of those stressful days and you *have a headache and just wish it would go away.* Well, I have and I do have something my doctor gave me for those times when I just know this one has the symptoms to become a migraine. Esgic-Plus works for me. Within about 20 minutes all signs of the on-coming headache are gone. Being frugal, I even cut the pill in half (as I've discovered that ½ works just as well as taking a whole pill), and then I heat a 2 cup measuring cup filled with water in the microwave for 2 ½ minutes. All microwaves heat a little different, but you are looking to get the water comfortably hot. I always make sure to eat a few crackers or 2-3 spoonfuls of yogurt to make sure I'm not putting medicine on an empty stomach. By then my hot water is ready and I pour it into the hot water bottle, lay the hot water bottle on the counter top next to the kitchen sink and carefully burp out the air before screwing in the cap. Then I head off to my room, climb under the covers and place the hot water bottle under my head and neck area. After a few minutes I move it to my forehead. Ah, the pain begins to melt away and I often fall off to sleep and wake up rested.

    The warmth is sooooooo soothing that almost immediately the headache starts to subside. If it's too hot move it to your forehead for a few seconds or a minute, and alternate a few times. You will feel the stress going away as you begin to relax. You can also use a paper towel between you and the hot water bottle if that is more comfortable. As it gets to a comfortable temperature, and the medicine is working you may find you drift off to sleep and wake up refreshed. If you don't have a hot water bottle, I highly recommend getting one. It travels with me and it is my best friend in a time of need!

- ❖ *The Family Life Conference* is another wonderful tool that many couples have discovered. You know, it is often said that *we take our cars into the shop more often than we take our marriages!* And, yes, they do need a tune up as we get "comfortable" with one another and forget how to date our mate! We also all come with some sort of baggage and without a doubt, we all know that men and women are wired differently from before birth with different DNA ... so don't be surprised if your marriage could use a "face lift," or a "wake-up call" ... because if you don't date your spouse, someone else would love to take on that role! Think back to the things you enjoyed before you got married and fan those embers to start a new flame that may need rekindling. Check it out: *www.familylife.com* and look for conferences in your area! You'll be glad you did. Make it a birthday present, a valentine's present, a just because present. Do it … and you'll be glad you did!

❖ Have your teenagers ever come home excited about **the latest movie that "everyone" is going to see** and they want your permission to go with the gang. I heard a story about a father who was presented with this scenario and he gave some very wise advice. He told them he would give them an answer the next day. Then he checked the website *www.pluggedin.com* (that he heard about on Focus on the Family) and made a batch of brownies. The website tells you the content of most any movie, noting if there is any bad language, violence, sex, etc. The teenagers excitedly showed up the next day and their father presented his answer this way. He said, "I have made you some very special brownies. They only have a little dog do in them, but you'll get used to it and won't notice it much. You see the movie you want to see has some garbage in it, and the more you watch stuff like that you will become numb to the contents and only be satisfied by more garbage. So, just like these brownies, if you are willing to eat some, you'll only get a little sick and may later acquire a taste for them and not notice the difference. Would you like to try them?" Needless to say, they got the point. They chose not to see the movie and not to eat the brownies!

❖ Have you ever had a piece of furniture that over the years was showing a variety of nicks and scratches and wished that you could replace it or figure out how to make it look better. Well, the other day I was looking at a bathroom wood grain cabinet that had a ton of scratches and reached for the bottle of liquid **Old English Scratch Cover**. I put some on a paper towel and began to work it into the wood. In seconds the scratches disappeared and the overall look was 100% better than it had been! I then moved to my coffee table that our Golden Lab/Belgian Sheppard pup many years ago had used for a teething ring! Once again the results were amazing and unless you really look closely, you would not recognize it as the same coffee table! Miracles never cease! Now I'm headed for the kitchen cupboards!

❖ Check this out for *Flight Upgrades*: *www.flightbliss.com* *How to Fly First Class for the Price of Coach* ... First Class Flyer. Send questions to: *mr.upgrade@flightbliss.com*

❖ *Kayak* ... I know that might sound like a funny name for a website for booking airline travel, but it brings all the others pretty much under one umbrella, if you will ... Check it out: *www.kayak.com* will take you to a website where you can look at the airline flights that you want on almost all the airline carriers. A few exceptions that are not included in the site are Southwest and Jet Blue.

❖ Have you ever seen someone across the room that you would like to get to know and missed the opportunity? I even danced with someone in Ocean City and somehow missed exchanging info to be back in contact. In talking with "the younger generation" who know all the latest techy possibilities, they encouraged me to look on FaceBook ... but he wasn't there. Then someone suggested that I look on *www.craigslist.com* under *Missed Connections* and see if he or someone he had told about our meeting knew that I was looking for him!

Nothing ventured, nothing gained! So here's what I posted. However, it reminds me once again that it is a lot easier to write down a phone number or an e-mail address so you don't have to wonder "if" you will ever meet that person again!!! Once again, an ounce of prevention is worth a pound of cure!!! Exchange phone numbers before you part ways!

washington, DC craigslist > personals > missed connections

Great Dancing with You, Dale from Pittsburg! - w4m (Ocean City, MD)

Dale from Pittsburg - You came up to our table and complimented me on my dancing. We danced together and somehow never exchanged info. We hoped you would come back to dance again the next evening. Would enjoy the opportunity to talk with you and get to know you!

If you read this, tell me the name of the place where we were dancing. All the best to you! Keep dancing - You are gifted. Location: Ocean City, MD

❖ The definition of a guy who is a *"HUNK"* looks something like this ...

   H Honest, Humble, and ... Handsome inside and out
   U Unbelievably talented, successful in what he does and he is a joy to know
   N Naturally fun to be around, sometimes funny, enjoys life, has a purpose and a dream and is not afraid to pursue it
   K Knows Jesus as his personal Lord and Savior, walks tall in his daily life, desires to grow in his walk with the Lord, and has fellowship and accountability with a few other Christian men to help him stand strong in a world without morals and values

❖ It's wonderful *being around people younger than you*, because they know how to make your cell phone work and how to get the pictures out of your digital camera and onto your computer, etc., etc!

❖ Have you ever *made the brilliant decision to move something from where it was and store it in a new place?* It might be a file in your filing cabinet, or something else around your home. Then when you go to look for it, do you find that you go to the place where it was originally? I do. Then I sit there and go where in the world was it that I moved it to during my brainstorm! Well, I've solved that insanity. I now make myself write a post-it note and put it in the original place telling me where I have placed it. I have even started a file on the computer noting original location and new location. Life is crazy enough without making myself crazy trying to remember where I put something during a brainstorm!!!

❖ Remember: *Salt adds flavor ... so be salt and light to those people God places in your world*. Gently speak into their lives if you see areas that need change and invite them to consider a different way to do something that has become a rut. Encourage them to change just one thing this week and each following week. Check out Matthew 5:13-16.

- **Looking for a book you can't seem to find???** Check out this website: *www.fetchbook.info*

- I have discovered that by Googling ***Boarders Marketplace*** I have been able to find used books that were not available on other websites, or the price was better at this website. My workbook cost me $1.04. Check it out if you need a slightly used book or workbook! Another resource is ***Books Squared***. They provide an extensive selection of cheap used books. My friend ordered a book that said it was in great condition and when she received it found that it was a perfectly new book for one cent! The shipping was $3.00 … but even so, it cost much less than paying the full price of $10.00 for a new book.

- ***Catch those Nasty Germs before they attack you!*** Did you know that most viruses hide in your colon until they are ready to spread throughout your body and make you feel sick? Think of it, a warm moist place (kind of like a Petri dish) where they can grow and congregate before spreading! Sooooo, the wise person will get rid of them within moments or the first few hours that you begin to notice that you don't feel well and avoid the hazard of coming down with a full-blown cough, cold, flu or other illness. So, if you believe that an ounce of prevention is worth a pound of cure here is what a wonderful homeopathic doctor friend told me to do.

    Keep powdered Vitamin C on hand. You can buy it at any vitamin store in your area and some pharmacies, Target, Walmart, or grocery store. The moment you notice you do not feel well, (that's the key … catch it Right Away!), put 5,000 milligrams of powdered Vitamin C in a small amount (2 to 3 inches) of water or juice (apple juice works well), and drink it down. Do the same thing again every 15 minutes for 1 hour. That's 4 times in 1 hour. Stay near the bathroom as it will flush your system, clean out your colon and take the nasty germs with it and you can flush them away! Amazingly enough, you will begin to feel much better real soon and never come down with the cold, virus, flu that had plans to knock you off your feet! Try it. It works. Catching it in the very early stages is the key. If you wait 2 or 3 days to try this, your probably tooooooo late!

❖ In a tight economy, have you ever considered *renting a room in your home*? There are many quality young people who are living away from home and working in your area. I place a notice on the bulletin board and on the Room Connection website at my church. It has been delightful having 2 and sometimes 3 young ladies in their 20's rent rooms in my 5 bedroom home. After having been a wife and a mom for many years, looking at 4 walls can be deafening! I need to hear *"laughter in the walls"* of this home. For many years, even when my husband was going to Westminster Seminary, we rented a room in our home to another seminary student. Now, through life's throw-away society, I find myself as a single mom of a wonderful college student who has just finished his biology pre-med degree in North Carolina! Life must go on … so renting rooms to quality gals has made this a warm, inviting home for them, and helps me keep my sanity!

Check your local newspaper to see what the going rates are for renting rooms and you will find that it will help you financially, and be a blessing to those who help to make your house feel like a home! I personally like to rent to gals in their 20's as they don't usually have "a lot of stuff" … including dining room tables, sofa's, etc. and they can decorate their room with their things. I've included my __Posting for a room__, and the __Questionnaire__ I use for a screening phone interview. If I like what I hear, I invite them to come for a visit to talk and see my home. I have also attached the __Housing Agreement__ I have used for years. My philosophy is that I do not need a "year's lease." If they are happy and I am happy, they will stay for at least a year and often longer! If it is not working … which has only happened once in many years of renting rooms in my home, then they give me … or I give them one month's notice and we part ways. Another thing to remember is that having your own business or renting a room in your home gives you added tax advantages to bring down the taxes you pay each year! A portion of your utilities, repairs, yard work, etc. become tax deductible. Now that's a Great Idea!

❖ *Mediator* – I never knew the real value of working with a mediator until I found myself in the middle of a divorce that I certainly did not want. Through our church we located a Christian man who was very good at helping each of us *"speak to one another in words the other could understand."* Now that's an art! I highly recommend looking into finding a Christian mediator if you are having trouble communicating or want a better marriage.

❖ **Peroxide** ... Who would have thought! It's great for:

- Killing a fungus on your toe. Did you know that thick toenails are an indication of a fungus? Soak a cotton ball with Peroxide and drip it around and under the toe nail, twice per day for two weeks and see the difference.
- Another great product is Tea Tree Oil. You can find it in your health food stores and local vitamin stores. Apply it twice per day and watch the fungus go away.
- White vinegar may work for you as well.

❖ *Measuring cup cleaning made easy*! Before you pour sticky substances into a measuring cup, fill with hot water. Dump out the hot water, but don't dry the cup. Next, add your ingredient, such as peanut butter, and watch how easily it comes right out. Amazing.

❖ Have you ever needed just *a little more frosting to finish your cake*? Actually, when you buy a container of cake frosting from the store, if you whip it with your mixer for a few minutes, you can double it in size. You can also add a little milk to thin it out. Now you can frost more cake/cupcakes, eat less sugar and there are less calories per serving.

❖ *Do you like a strong garlic taste or just a touch*? Add garlic immediately to a recipe if you want a light taste of garlic and at the end of the recipe if your want a stronger taste of garlic.

❖ *When you cook rice, does it often stick to the bottom of the pan?* Daniella from Ecuador showed me that by putting a teaspoon of oil in the pan with the water and rice keeps it from sticking!

- ❖ *Fiber ...* If you're not getting enough fiber in your diet, know that you can buy **Cold-Milled Organic Ground Flax Seeds** at Walmart and sprinkle it on your cereal. Also, *Fiber-sure* which they now call **Clear & Natural** is a clear-mixing fiber supplement which is flavor free, grit free, and non-thickening. It mixes easily into food or drinks without altering its taste or texture. Add a heaping teaspoon to cereal, anything you cook, breakfast smoothies, soup, yogurt, salad dressing, stir-fry or just mix it in with your favorite beverage. **Clear & Natural** is made by Metamucil. If you can't find it in your local stores, you can call them with questions at 800 / 525-2855. If for some reason this does not work for you, try taking Senokot tablets (a natural laxative) in the evening before bedtime and using it alone or with the fiber should definitely work your system on a daily basis. Everyone's system is different so you will have to work with it to see what combination works best for you.

- ❖ Your *clothes dryer lint filter* may need attention! Before your heating unit goes out on your dryer, you may want to be aware of this! Even though you may clean it out after every load, and it "looks clean," there may be a waxy film that has built up from using dryer sheets. Take the filter over to the sink and run hot water over it. Notice if the hot water just sits on top of the mesh screen of the lint filter! If it doesn't go through at all, the holes are clogged!

Dryer sheets cause a film over that mesh and that's what burns out the heating unit. You can't SEE the film, but it's there. It's what is in the dryer sheets to make your clothes soft and static free ... that nice fragrance too. You know how dryer sheets feel waxy when you take them out of the box ... well this stuff builds up on your clothes and on your lint screen. This is also what causes dryer units to potentially burn your house down!

The best way to keep your dryer working for a very longtime (and to keep your electric bill lower) is to take the filter out and wash it with hot soapy water and an old toothbrush (or other brush) at least every six months. As with most things, a little maintenance may extend the life of your dryer at least twice as long! How about that!?! Learn something new everyday!

Check it out. If you are like me and use the dryer sheets, try running water through your lint filter and see if it puddles up or runs through easily. Then wash the lint filter with warm soapy water and a nylon brush for about 15-30 seconds. Then rinse it and the water should run right thru the screen!

❖ <u>*Ladies, in the middle of winter or ... anytime, do you like looking like you have a tan?*</u> Well, try purchasing a foundation that is a shade or two darker than your skin tone. Wet your fingers before applying the foundation to your face and put it on lightly. It will add just enough color that you and everyone else will think that you have been to the islands!

❖ Have you ever wanted to ***Attend a Conference,*** but it didn't fit in your budget? ... Hum, well put on your thinking cap. They always need behind the scenes folks to help with the bookstore or pre conference nametags and books and papers to handout ... Soooooo, be proactive and call the sponsors of the conference and volunteer to help out. ***Often for being willing to serve while you are there, you will be able to attend the conference for FREE or at a very reduced rate.***

❖ Have you ever stopped in to visit your local health food store or Whole Foods grocery store and *asked some questions about what they would recommend for your various health issues.* Well, if you haven't, I know that you will be amazed at the various herbs that are available to treat many conditions. Also herbs can often be much better for you than taking medicine that has some awful side effects. There is a wonderful book called: <u>***Prescription for Nutritional Healing***</u> by James F & Phyllis A. Balch that will give you insights into what you can do to help various conditions. Check it out. Now that's a Great Idea!

❖ Experience visiting with a Nutritionist: Siliva tests can show you if you are <u>*gluten intolerant*</u>. Who would have ever known? If you are, than you should not eat any white flour, wheat flour, rye, barley, and possibly oats as they could be a cause for constipation. Gluten intolerant people cannot process all foods that others can and it can have various negative effects on your body. If you have food issues, check it out.

❖ *Dancing* ... If you have comfortable shoes for dancing, but they don't slide very well on a wooden dance floor, ***put a piece of gray duck tape on the front sole of your shoes*** and you will glide across the floor! I've even seen folks put duck tape on the bottom of tennis shoes. Of course, if you haven't taken any dance lessons, you may want to contact your local community center and learn a few steps to help you get in the groove! If you dance often, dance shoes can be found on-line at various websites. One really nice feature I discovered with both websites listed below is that shoes that look like they buckle actually have a notch that the buckle sits in to hold the shoe on tight, but you don't have to buckle and unbuckle the shoe each time you take it on and off! Very Nice Feature! I found some of the best prices and quality at Dance 4 Less, ***www.dance4less.com*** and HSE Discount Dancewear which offers shoes and accessories at **www.houstonsalsaevents.com** .

❖ *Dancing is for two* ... How many times have you attended a dance and sat and wished you were out there on the floor ***dancing the night away*** ... but haven't been asked to dance??? Well, the truth is ... guys are more "shy" than you think! After speaking with many, many guys, they assured me that they are easily intimidated by a table full of ladies and wouldn't think of approaching your table to ask one of you to dance. So, what's the solution??? If you want to dance:

- Stand up and walk towards the edge of the dance floor ... Be available to dance!
- Smile and look like you are enjoying yourself ... you are now much more approachable!
- If so inclined, sway and tap your feet to the music
- If you see someone pass by that you would like to dance with ... simply stretch out your right hand about waist level, look them in the eye, and say: ***Do you like to dance?*** I have never had a gentleman refuse such a gentle, welcoming offer ... unless they truly don't know how to dance and then you just smile and slowly move around the room, smiling and looking for a potential dance partner. A smile goes a long way.
- Relax, smile, and extend your right hand to a gentleman who is holding up the wall! You will find yourself enjoying dancing the night away to the melody of delightful danceable music!

- Many a very good dancer is shy to ask a woman to dance ... so once again, while you are "on tour around the room," if you see someone you would like to dance with that is standing against the wall or leaning on the banister ... (it's just a dance, it's not a commitment for life!), smile, reach out your right hand, ask: "Do you like to dance?" ... and more often than not you will find yourself enjoying the dance and meeting a new friend. Often the gentlemen will thank you for getting him out on the dance floor! Strangers are only friends you haven't met yet!

Yvonne,

I used to sit on the sidelines at sooooooo many dances and sometimes only danced one or two dances the whole evening. Then I decided there must be a way to switch this up ... especially if I had paid more than a few $$$ to get into the dance. As they say: **Necessity is the mother of invention... and I decided to do something different ... because we all know "the definition of insanity is to do the same thing over and over again and expect different results!"** *It took me a long time to figure out what to do different ... and then it was sooooo easy ...*

- *Stand up*
- *Smile*
- *Walk forward and go up to someone and say: Do you dance? ... Seems rather harmless and has had amazing results!*

Actually, I danced sooooo much last night and we stayed till the very end so I am a bit of a zombie today! Got up early as the sun was beaming in my window and after a couple of hours of being up this morning went back to bed and slept for another hour! I may think I'm 37 ... but my body is reminding me that I'm not! Ha! An Advil with breakfast didn't hurt either!

Hugs,
Shirley

PS: Practice smiling and extending your hand about waist level in the mirror and saying: Do you dance? Tee Hee

- Do your feet need more *cushion* than sandals provide? Often you can find *insoles* at the dollar store and cut them to fit your sandals. Your feet will thank you! If your sandals have a toe piece that separates your big toe, just cut a line from the edge of the insole to the toe piece divider and insert your insole cushion around it. Once you have it cut to size, glue it in place for added comfort.

- *Old Musty Smells in old dresser drawers or other furniture* … Spray Febreze in each drawer of the piece of furniture, then place dryer sheets (yes, the kind you use for your laundry) in each drawer. Come back in about an hour and you will be amazed!!! Ah, fresh and ready to use!

- When our dog became ill, he threw up all over the new carpet in the middle of the night. I wasn't sure the stain and blood would ever come out, but was delighted when I tried *Woolite's Spot & Stain Carpet Cleaner – OXY DEEP*. There is not even a trace of the stain and the crème carpet looks fresh again.

- *Sandpaper vs. moist sponge!* After you spackle a wall as you prepare to paint it, instead of waiting for the spackling to dry and sanding the spackled spot(s) … take a moist paper towel or *moist sponge and smooth out the spot(s) while it is wet*. Then there is no need to go find the sandpaper and use all that elbow grease while trying to sand it once it dries! Now That's a Great Idea!!!

- *Buying a GPS:* I wrote some friends and asked for suggestions on which GPS they would recommend. I mentioned that if I could choice the voice, I would like an Australian guy voice, kind of like the Geico gecko! The accent gives me a chuckle, so it would be fun listening to his prompts. Here were some of the responses I received:

    - ✓ Walt wrote back and said his GPS features "Mag the Hag" and he would not recommend her, but she does keep him alert! Too funny!
    - ✓ Ha! I knew having an Australian guy voice was a good idea. My Australian guy would say … That's right dearie. Cheerio!

- ✓ Another person said to check on YouTube. I would have never thought of this, but they say they have videos on everything … even how to choose a GPS … and learning how to string pearls! Amazing!
- ✓ GPS.......Garmin was the forerunner and first in the navigation area of GPS. Tom says they are user friendly and have easy to understand prompts.

❖ *Extended flexible vacuum hose* … To get something out of a heat register or under the fridge add an empty paper towel roll or empty gift wrap roll to your vacuum. This makes the hose more flexible so you can bend or flatten it to get in narrow openings.

❖ Use your *hair conditioner to shave your legs*. It's cheaper than shaving cream and leaves your legs really smooth. It's also a great way to use up the conditioner you bought but didn't like when you tried it in your hair.

❖ *If ants are a problem*, try these:

  - Sprinkle cornmeal where you see ants. They eat it, take it "home," can't digest it, so it kills them. It may take a week or so, especially if it rains, but it works and you don't have the worry about pets or small children being harmed!
  - Boric Acid can be bought at the dollar store and it works too.
  - Dry powdered soap detergent also works.
  - My favorite is using Lysol Disinfectant spray. Wherever you see ants, spray the area and the liquid gets on their feet.

❖ To *keep squirrels from eating your plants*, sprinkle your plants with cayenne pepper. The cayenne pepper doesn't hurt the plant and the squirrels won't come near it.

❖ Michael suggested this … but I haven't actually tried it! If you need the trees in your yard trimmed and can't afford to spend $300 or so per tree to get it professionally done, post an ad on Craig's List saying *Free Firewood and Mulch* … you cut it, haul it, mulch it and it's yours! It's a win-win scenario! I get my trees trimmed and you get the firewood. Now you may want to have them sign a waiver before they climb your tree saying that you are not liable. You may also only want to trim trees that are not near your house in case a branch falls the wrong way!!! Hum.

Chapter 11

✓ **<u>Quotable Quotes</u>** … Some serious, some to make you smile, and some to tickle your funny bone! Some I received in e-mails that have no known author and some are my own. Those with known authors are noted below.

- ❖ If your parents didn't have any children, chances are you won't either!

- ❖ If the cow doesn't give milk, sell him! (He's a bull … and bulls don't give milk.)

- ❖ Two natures live within my breast, the one I feed will dominate! Think about it and act accordingly!

- ❖ It's not the size of the gale, but the set of the sail that determines the direction of your ship!

- ❖ Beware of your choices: The mind justifies what the heart desires!

- ❖ God's Word will keep you from sin … Or … Sin will keep you from God's Word and God's will!

- In the business world the bottom line is profit or loss. In the real world the bottom line is saved or lost. Why not consider making a decision today that will affect your life for eternity. Consider accepting Jesus Christ as your personal Savior and secure your place in eternity!

- God's tool box – Read it, memorize it, write it on your heart, act on it, and share it with others.

- If you try to use the wrong tool to fix something, it will certainly take longer and may not work at all! Know what's in your tool box and assess the need before you start the project. If you get in trouble, phone a friend!

- Life does have a way of having many chapters, and hopefully they are mostly filled with at least one nugget of wisdom / happiness / truth that will make us better people for the next chapter!

- Courtesy is owed – Respect is earned – Love is given!

- You don't stop laughing when you grow old, you grow old because you stop laughing!

- "The naked truth is always better than the best dressed lie." Ann Landers

- An older woman was concerned because she was having trouble remembering things. Her daughter wisely said, Mom, just don't forget to laugh.

- A man of words and not of deeds is like a garden full of weeds. – Anonymous

- As He is the potter and I am the clay, I pray He will mold me and make me usable for His purpose! Fill me, walk beside me, lead me. Lord help me to see life through Your eyes!

- God's invitation is personal! No greater invitation has ever been given to the human race. Think about it. You must make a choice to receive His Free Gift of eternal life. It cost Jesus His life. He came to save sinners and offer them forgiveness, a hope, and a future very different than their past.

- ❖ "You have brains in your head. You have feet in your shoes. You can steer yourself in any direction you choose. You're on your own. And you know what you know. You are the guy who'll decide where to go." – Dr. Seuss

- ❖ "If your work speaks for itself, don't interrupt." – Henry J. Kaiser

- ❖ You are a letter from Christ – read by all. So be careful how you live!

- ❖ "People may doubt what you say, but they will believe what you do." – Lewis Cass

- ❖ "The difference between the right word and the almost right word is the difference between lightening and a lightening bug." – Mark Twain

- ❖ Two older ladies were walking and talking … To stay young, the doctor said to Exercise and Eat the Right Foods. What?! I thought he said Accessorize and Buy Nice Shoes!

- ❖ "Never apologize for showing feeling. When you do so, you apologize for the truth." – Benjamin Disraeli

- ❖ "What lies behind us and what lies before us are tiny matters compared to what lies within us." – Oliver Wendell Holmes

- ❖ New friends are just people you haven't met yet! Sooooo, go and make some new friends!

- ❖ Your friends will not always go with you… but there are times when you should go.

- Remember to stop and smell the flowers along life's way. When you are gone from your job, be assured they will find someone else to fill your shoes and life will go on. How will your kids and your spouse remember you? Were you there for them?

- Ladies … dress modestly! It is attractive and honoring to the minds and hearts of the guys who you want to be gentlemen!

- Disappointment is inevitable … Misery is a choice!

- Some succeed because they are destined to, but most succeed because they are determined to!

- Remember …. The Titanic … The ship that wouldn't sink! It sunk. The life boats were only ½ full. Why did some people stay on the boat? The said, "It can't sink … it will come back" … and they drowned!

- "The most powerful weapon in the world is truth!" Ravi Zacharias

- "The strength of a nation lies in the homes of its people." Abraham Lincoln

- "Be more concerned with your character than your reputation, because your character is what you really are, while your reputation is merely what others think you are." John Robert Wooden, UCLA Basketball Coach Emeritus

- Everyone wants to be needed, wanted, and matter to somebody. We soar inside and well up with confidence to walk forward when we sense we have dignity, worth, value, love, respect, forgiveness and a healing as only Jesus can provide.

- "After I set out to refute Christianity intellectually and couldn't, I came to the conclusion the Bible was true and Jesus Christ was God's Son." Josh McDowell

- "If Jesus Christ was who He claimed to be, and He did die on a cross at a point of time in history, then, for all history past and all history future it is relevant because that is the very focal point for forgiveness and redemption." Josh McDowell

❖ "We have a right to believe whatever we want, but not everything we believe is right." Ravi Zacharias

❖ "These days its not just that the line between right and wrong has been made unclear, today Christians are being asked by our culture today to erase the lines and move the fences, and if that were not bad enough, we are being asked to join in the celebration cry by those who have thrown off the restraints religion had imposed upon them. It is not just that they ask that we accept, but they now demand of us to celebrate it too." Ravi Zacharias

Chapter 12

✓ **Food for Thought …**

- ❖ Ann Graham Lotz wrote: "When you feel helpless, trust Him. I don't doubt His love and commitment toward me, and I know He has His best in mind for me. Are you doubting? Read John Chapter 11. Jesus enters into our grief."

- ❖ Know that God will make a way when there seems to be no way. With God's strength, He will make a way. Listen to this song on You Tube by Don Moen. God Will Make A Way … *http://www.youtube.com/watch?v=1zo3fJYtS-o*

- ❖ There are no new truths – just new personal applications

- ❖ Quality Christian Friendships: I admire you as a woman with Godly principals, love you as a sister, treasure you as a friend, and count myself very fortunate to have you in my life.

- ❖ Anxiety robs you of your joy and stifles you from being able to move ahead.

- ❖ *Write a tribute to your parents.* It may just be the most "treasured gift" you ever give them. You may want to frame it or present it at a birthday, anniversary, Mother's Day or Father's Day. You can get a CD from Dennis Rainey of Family Life Today for ideas of how to proceed. As a parent, there is no greater gift than words written on a page stating your love, affection, appreciation, affirmation, struggles, and thankfulness for their sacrifices and care for you as a child, young adult and now peer. Remember, maybe your parents didn't have the best example in their parents, but they very possibly did the best with what they knew at the time. Heal the wounds and build bridges while you still have time.

- ❖ *Salt & Light* … Colossians 4:6 let your speech be seasoned with salt so you will know how you should respond to each other.

- ❖ *Ginger Root* …Chop up a piece of ginger root in a food processor. Put it in a container and cover with cream sherry. Store in refrigerator and it will last a very long time. Try a little of this mixture on meat dishes or fish.

- ❖ Recipes for you ….

  - ✓ <u>*Shirley's Delicious Carrot Bread*</u>

    - Mix Together …
      - 1 ½ cups sugar
      - 2 teaspoons salt
      - 2 teaspoons vanilla
      - 1 cup cooking oil
      - 3 eggs

    - Then add these dry items to the above mixture …
      - 2 teaspoons cinnamon
      - 2 teaspoons baking soda
      - 2 cups flour … you may use white or whole wheat or mix a combination

- Now add these items ...
  - ¼ cup chopped nuts
  - 2 cups grated carrots
  - 1 cup raisins
  - ½ cup coconut

- Note: The batter will be very thick by this point, but your bread will be very moist.
- Bake in well-greased loaf pans at 350 degrees for 45 minutes. Makes two loafs

✓ *<u>Barb's Coconut Bars</u>*

- 1 stick margarine melted
- 1 1/3 cups Graham Cracker crumbs
- 6 oz chocolate chips
- 6 oz butterscotch chips
- 1 cup flaked coconut
- 1 cup pecans or walnuts
- 1 cup Eagle brand condensed milk

- Butter 9 x 13 pan
- Blend crumbs and margarine, then pat into pan
- Layer next 4 ingredients
- Drizzle milk over the top
- Bake at 325 degrees for 20-25 minutes

✓ *<u>Mint Brownie Treat</u>*

Make brownies as directed. Melt Andes mints in double broiler and pour over warm brownies. Let it set for a wonderful minty frosting.

✓ *Peanut Butter Pie*

- ½ cup Peanut Butter
- 3 oz. Cream Cheese
- 1 cup 10X Sugar
- 2 cups Cool Whip
- 1 Graham Cracker OR Chocolate Pie Shell

- Cream peanut butter and cream cheese together
- Add sugar & Cool Whip … Mix thoroughly
- Pour into pie shell. Refrigerate. Enjoy!!!

✓ *Apple Caramel Nut Dessert*

Leftover snickers bars from Halloween make a delicious dessert. Simply chop them up with the food chopper. Peel, core and slice a few apples. Place them in a baking dish and sprinkle the chopped candy bars over the apples. Bake at 350 for 15 minutes!!! Serve alone or with vanilla ice cream. Yummm!

✓ *Broiled Sesame Ginger Teriyaki Salmon*

For easy clean-up, place a piece of aluminum foil on a tray, then add the salmon
Drizzle Sesame & Ginger Teriyaki over the salmon
Sprinkle on Jane's Crazy Mixed-Up Seasonings
Sprinkle on Sweet Basil
Broil or Bake 15 to 20 minutes. Your fish should be moist and flake easily when done.

✓ *Teriyaki Garlic Chicken*

Drizzle Teriyaki Marinade over chicken, sprinkle with minced garlic, sweet basil and Jane's Krazy Mixed Up Seasonings. Bake for 45 minutes and enjoy!

✓ *Zesty Vegetable Pasta*

Use McCormick's Salad Supreme Seasoning, add pasta and a variety of your choice of colorful vegetables (yellow or green zucchini; green, yellow or red peppers; slivered/shredded carrots, cherry tomatoes, sliced cucumber) and raisins or craisins (cranberry raisins) for a great pasta salad.. The recipe is on the back of the Salad Supreme container. Great for picnics, serve cold.

✓ *Marty's Veggie Burgers*

- 1½ lbs ground beef or turkey
- 1 cup shredded potatoes
- 1 cup shredded carrots
- 1 cup chopped onion
- 2 tsp salt
- 1 TBL Poultry Seasoning
- 2 eggs

Mix all ingredients together and form into hamburger patties. Brown in a skillet, on the grill or in the oven until cooked through. Enjoy!

✓ *Easy Turkey Sausage Manicotti*

Have you ever wanted to make a quick lasagna? Well, here it is with all the same ingredients, but with a variation on how you put it together.

- 1 lb turkey sausage
- 1 large onion
- 2 cups cottage cheese (16 oz)
- 1 jar spaghetti sauce
- 1 cup shredded part-skim Mozzarella cheese (4 oz)
- 1 package manicotti shells (8 oz) - Approximately 4 inch shells
- Jane's Crazy Mixed Up Salt (or other salt spice)
- Sweet Basil
- Oregano or Italian Spices

Directions:
- Combine sausage (uncooked), cottage cheese, most of the jar of spaghetti sauce, half of the bag of Mozzarella cheese, salt, basil and oregano
- Lightly grease 9 x 13 pan and pour shells (uncooked) into pan
- Cover shells with sausage mixture
  - Top with remaining spaghetti sauce
- Cover with aluminum foil and bake at 350 degrees for 55-60 minutes – The sausage will cook, shells will soften and absorb the flavors, cheese will melt.
- Uncover, sprinkle top of dish with remaining Mozzarella cheese, a little basil and oregano
- Bake for 8 – 10 minutes longer
- Let stand 5 minutes ... Enjoy!

✓ ***Shirley's Florentine Chicken Ring***

- 3 – 4 pieces of cooked chicken (1 cup) cut up in small pieces or you can use 1 can 10 ounce chunk chicken
- 1 large onion, sautéed in butter or olive oil
- 1 pkg. of frozen spinach, thawed and well drained
- 1/3 cup mayonnaise
- ½ cup red bell pepper, chopped

- 1 tablespoon crushed garlic
- 1 package (8 oz) cream cheese
- ½ cup cherry tomatoes, sliced
- 1 teaspoon lemon zest
- 1 teaspoon Jane's Crazy Mixed Up Seasoning
- ½ teaspoon sweet basil
- 1 teaspoon Dijon mustard
- 1/8 teaspoon ground pumpkin pie spice
- 2 packages (8 ounces each) refrigerated crescent rolls

Preheat oven to 375 degrees. Mix all ingredients in large bowl (except for crescent rolls) and mix well.

Open both packages of crescent rolls and place wide ends of triangles overlapping slightly in the center so they form a circle on a pizza pan with the points of the triangles of dough hanging over the edge of the pan. There should be a 5 inch diameter opening in the center of the pizza pan.

Scoop chicken mixture onto the widest end of each triangle of dough. Then bring the points of the dough up over the filling and tuck under wide ends of dough at the center of the ring. The filling will not be completely covered. Bake for 20-25 minutes or until golden brown. Delicious, colorful and festive!

❖ *Now, here's a recipe for each new day* ....

1. Eat breakfast like a king, lunch like a prince and dinner like a college kid with a maxed out charge card!

2. Take a 10-30 minute walk every day. And while you walk, smile. It is the ultimate anti-depressant!

3. When you wake up in the morning complete the following statements: "My purpose is to _____ today. I am thankful for _____."

4. Eat more foods that grow on trees and plants and eat less food that is manufactured in plants.

5. Drink green tea and plenty of water. Eat blueberries, wild Alaskan salmon, broccoli, almonds & walnuts.

6. Sit in silence for at least 10 minutes each day. Talk to God about what is going on in your life.

7. The foods on the outer isles of most grocery stores are usually the healthy choices, i.e. a variety of fruits, vegetables, chicken, turkey and fish.

8. Try to make at least three people smile each day.

9. Don't waste your precious energy on gossip, vampires, issues of the past, negative thoughts or things you cannot control. Instead invest your energy in the positive present moment!

10. Life isn't fair, but it's still good!

11. Life is too short to waste time hating anyone.

12. Don't take yourself so seriously. No one else does.

13. You are not so important that you have to win every argument. Agree to disagree.

14. Make peace with your past so it won't spoil the present.

15. Don't compare your life to others. You have no idea what their journey is all about.

16. No one is in charge of your happiness except you.

17. Frame every so-called disaster with these words: In five years will this matter?

18. Forgive everyone for everything. Refusing to forgive just keeps you in a self-made jail and everyone else is living free of worry about that which may give you an ulcer or worse!

19. What other people think of you is none of your business.

20. However good or bad a situation is, it will change.

21. Your job won't take care of you when you are sick. Your friends will. Stay in touch!!!

22. Envy is a waste of time. You already have all you need.

23. Each night before you go to bed, complete the following statements: I am thankful for _____. Today I accomplished _____.

24. Remember that you are too blessed to be stressed.

25. When you are feeling down, start listing your many blessings. You'll be smiling before you know it.

God's Blessings to you!!!!!!!!!!!!!!!!

The Letter

Dear Friend,

How are you? I just had to send a note to tell you how much I care about you.

I saw you yesterday as you were talking with your friends. I waited all day hoping you would want to talk with me too. I gave you a sunset to close your day and a cool breeze to rest you – and I waited. You never came. It hurt me – but I still love you because I am your friend.

I saw you sleeping last night and longed to touch your brow so I spilled moonlight upon your face. Again I waited, wanting to rush down so we could talk. I have so many gifts for you! You awoke and rushed off to work. My tears were in the rain.

If you would only listen to me! I love you! I try to tell you in blue skies and in the quiet green grass. I whisper in the leaves on the trees and breathe it in colors of flowers, shout it to you in mountain streams, give the birds love songs to sing. I clothe you with warm sunshine and perfume the air with nature scents. My love for you is deeper than the ocean, and bigger than the biggest need in your heart!

Ask me! Talk with me! Please don't forget me. I have so much to share with you! I won't hassle you any further. It is YOUR decision. I have chosen you and I will wait ---

I love you.

Your friend,

Jesus

I was given a picture frame with this letter. Author unknown.

Chapter 13

✓ **<u>Just for Fun, Encouragement, Things to Brighten Your Day, Every Day!</u>**

In this chapter I have included a variety of websites for you to visit to brighten your day! Some are funny, some are delightful, some are thought provoking, some heart touching, and some will lift your spirits and make you smile.

<u>Double click on the attachment or highlight it and put it in your Internet search bar, turn up your speakers and enjoy.</u> On some you can click through the slides by placing your mouse at the bottom left of your computer screen and clicking on the right arrow. Over the years I have received these in e-mails that were passed along. Enjoy!

- *"I Believe" ...*   This is one of the <u>most beautiful and meaningful</u> streaming videos ever created. You will want to keep it as a cherished treasure. Be sure your speakers are on **http://www.andiesisle.com/creation/magnificent.html**

- *This is so beautiful ... Did you ever wonder what's in the middle?*
  http://show.zoho.com/public/kirklandj/TheBibleDV-pps

- *This is inspiring, funny and good food for thought! What's the music in your heart?*
  http://www.youtube.com/watch?v=bYI_aOyCn9Y

- *Complete ... A wonderful message to encourage your day, lift your spirits and give you hope! Click on the link, sit back and turn up your sound.*
  http://www.youtube.com/watch?v=rNYc5El60PI&feature=related

- *Underwater Fantasy*
  The Amazing Beauty of Underwater Creation! A World All It's Own!
  http://www.youtube.com/watch?v=NKvZRdnR8wc&feature=related

- *Dog owners will chuckle at this one! Breakfast at Ginger's - Golden Retriever Dog eats with hands!*
  http://www.youtube.com/watch?v=HaAVZ2yXDBo

- *These may be the most unusual vacation spots!*
  http://www.youtube.com/watch?v=KTr6gItuEkE

- *The Meaning of Easter ... Watch this artist!*
  The following from CBN.com
  http://www.cbn.com/special/discovereaster/index.aspx?cpid=DE1003301

- *Fighter Pilots ... I'm Alive*
  http://www.youtube.com/watch?v=JiHG167WiDE

- *4 Elements - I'm Alive.*
  http://elsipogtog.ning.com/video/4-elements-im-alive-celine

- *You never know where you will find a friend. Animal lovers will enjoy this.*
  http://www.youtube.com/watch?v=JiHG167WiDE

- *Nature lovers will enjoy this version by Louis Armstrong*
  http://www.youtube.com/watch?v=RAZqjsSZphE&feature=related

- *This is so much of what life really is ... life on a train ride ...*
  http://www.youtube.com/watch?v=A__BItnzJb4

- *God Will Make A Way ... When there seems to be no way - Don Moen*
  http://www.youtube.com/watch?v=1zo3fJYtS-o

- *Gloriously beautiful photographs, as well as inspiring words.*
  This is absolutely beautiful
  http://www.youtube.com/watch?v=oQxd4sDOTKU

- *The Wise Old Man* - A man of 92 years who takes great care in his appearance, is moving into an old people's home ...
  www.slideshare.net/muneer/wise-old-man-36661

- *The Dash ... How will you live your life?* From the day you are born until the day they put an end date on your tombstone, what will your dash say to others?
  http://www.thedashmovie.com/

- *Have patience with your elders ...*
  http://www.youtube.com/watch?v=y381DEn5Ku0&feature=related

- *Beautiful Pictures ... Some will make you smile and warm your heart ... while others will take your breath away!!!*
  http://www.youtube.com/watch?v=hMTs7mEi6m0

- *A different kind of check-up ...*
  http://www.youtube.com/watch?v=xbXIIOWQssM

- *The Interview With God*
  http://www.theinterviewwithgod.com/popup-frame.html

- *Cardboard Testimonies*
  http://www.youtube.com/watch?v=RvDDc5RB6FQ

- *Beautiful Quotes to Live By ... Ah, the things we so easily forget!*
  http://www.youtube.com/watch?v=OPZr6CYyOGA&feature=related

- *If you find yourself as only 2 men on an island, what would you pray for?*
  http://www.youtube.com/watch?v=ko_VSKn1DAE&feature=related

- *Aren't you glad god gave us color ...*
  http://www.youtube.com/watch?v=oRoGlg1GdGA

- *When you say ... I Can't Solve This ... God Says ...*
  http://www.youtube.com/watch?v=GujApxlxX0I&feature=related

- *<u>Amazing Grace – II Divo</u>* ... The Four Tenors ... Sit back take it in!
  http://www.youtube.com/results?search_query=amazing+grace+il+divo&aq=9

- *Painter ... Watch all the way to the end and you won't believe your eyes!*
  http://www.youtube.com/watch?v=8M4_IlbaZHA

Chapter 14

✓ **Suggestions for Overall Health**

❖ *Plant New Seeds Today!* .... "**All the flowers of all your tomorrows are in the seeds of today!**" It's important to plant some new seeds by getting out and meeting some new people. Look in your local paper, in your church bulletin, on a website like www.meetup.com that lists groups of various activities and find a new group to visit. It will expand your horizons, nurture you and change your world ... and it just may lead to knowing about other activities as you talk together and get to know "strangers" ... who are just "friends" you haven't met yet!!!

- Decide on a healthy attitude, mindset, balance in life

- Develop your prayer time and spiritual growth

- Meet new people

- Get paperwork in order

All The Flowers Of All The Tomorrows Are In The Seeds Of Today

- If you're stuck, seek out an anxiety or anti-depression program or a counselor to help you through and be supported by others going through similar situations. Remember, you are not alone in this struggle. Others before you have paved the way so you don't have to reinvent the wheel (so to speak) to find the way out of depression. Learn from others and remember to get the help you need in this season of your life so you can begin the recovery process and start to live again.

- Remember, You are not alone … others before you have paved the way. Learn from others and get the help you need to live again. For more information, contact Focus on the Family, *www.focusonthefamily.com* or a local counselor or doctor. Start on the road to success, confidence and peace of mind.

- Recognize where you are and believe that tomorrow can be different.

- Anxiety robs you of your life and stifles you from being able to move ahead.

- Eat healthy – Minimize caffeine and sugars (both cause extreme changes in your glucose levels).

- Exercise daily – Critical to help remove toxins from the body. Exercise will help you sleep better, and increase your metabolism which will increase your energy level. Exercise increases blood flow and lung capacity. If you don't like going to the gym, consider a brisk walk, swimming or a bicycle ride. Have you thought about going dancing or learning to dance?

- Drink lots of water.

- Self-Talk: What you say to yourself will effect your energy level. Negative feelings trigger negative responses in your body. Positive feelings promote a sense of wellbeing.

- We often ask … What if? However, we are where we are … so begin setting goals for your future and work towards them every day.

❖ *<u>Overcoming Panic Attacks</u>*

- Give yourself permission to feel anxious. Ask yourself what's really bothering me right now? Am I obsessing over something?

- Give yourself permission. Ask yourself, why am I using them to set myself up for anxiety?

- Use positive self-talk.

- Get busy. Use that energy to charge your batteries. Play with the kids, clean out a closet.

- Laugh at yourself.

- Lucinda Basset has a very helpful series that I found helpful in finding my way out of depression. Listening to the tapes helped me to identify some of the causes of my depression and climb above the depression. Do you realize that it could be that you are giving someone else power over your emotions? Why are you allowing them to control your emotions? Realize that they don't deserve that power. Choose to redirect your priorities and reclaim your sanity.

- Listen to uplifting music, make friends with positive people (not those who bring you down), watch positive – not negative depressing things on TV (if you watch it at all)!

❖ *<u>Healing ADD & ADHD</u>* ... Much research has been done and Dr. Daniel Amen has some very interesting information in his book **<u>Healing ADD - ADHD</u>** that you will find very interesting. Studies have been done on the brain to see how it functions and pictures are presented in the book for you to see for yourself. *www.amenclinic.com*

❖ *<u>Building Lasting Relationships – Good Food for Thought - Seminar with Johnnie Parker</u>*

  - Express Yourself – Be clear. Don't assume someone can read your mind.

  - FM – Feeling Mode ... AM – Action / Analytical Mode ... Static on the line.

  - Insightful phrases: You Always, You Never, Why don't you?, Why did you?

  - Learn to speak in pictures. Word pictures help us visualize what we are saying.

  - Men are energized by "respect." Women are energized by "love."

  - Letter writing – Develop this skill to express your thoughts.

- The heart of the righteous studies how to answer.   Proverbs 15:28

- The way to the heart is through the ear and your actions. Does what they hear match up with what you actually do?

- Listen with your eyes – focus on what the other person is saying.

- Listen with your head – concentrate on what is being said.

- Listen with your lips so that your speech conveys that you have truly heard what was said.

- Statistics show 7% of the input we receive is through words, 55% visual is heard, 38% vocal is heard.

- Clarify what you say and hear – "Are you saying ………..?"

- Missing Pieces of the puzzle cause confusion. Say: "Let me repeat back to you what I think I heard you say." The person will feel understood or correct the part you misunderstood or they forgot to state! Either way, the missing puzzle pieces will be discovered and you will better understand each other.

- Paraphrasing (echo).. "What I am hearing you say is ..." or "It seems that you feel ..."

- Affirmation … "I can see that you feel …" or "Do you feel … ?"

- Conflict styles

  > Aggressive – Lion – Roars, fighter, must win, King of the Jungle, honest, sometimes brutal – Honesty without love, direct – You know where you stand. They go for the jugular!

  > Passive – Ostrich – What's wrong? … Nothing! What they really mean is …

"I can't believe they don't know what's going on." Indirect – "I don't want to talk." They need to learn to have the courage to speak the truth in love. Hit and run communication.

> <u>Assertive</u> – Porcupine – Honest but sometimes with harshness. Truth is love. We feel mad because we feel hurt, misunderstood, fearful, frustrated. WE can't make something happen. We feel powerless.

- Unhealthy extremes – Allowing anger to churn

- Depression is anger turned inward.

- Proverbs 12:37 – Anxiety in the heart makes the heart sick.

- Signs and symptoms of stuffed anger. It takes a lot to make me angry.

- Rage – Physical expression of stuffed anger. Blow up.

- Be aware of what you are feeling … What is churning in you?

- Resist blaming others for your feelings.

- Clarify what is causing you to feel angry.

- Decide to express anger in a healthy way.

<u>Forgiveness does not mean ….</u>

- I forget how you hurt me. But it does mean choosing not to play the tape over and over.

- It does not mean I am quick to rebuild trust after emotional damage. You must demonstrate trustworthy behavior.

- That the pain and hurt will somehow suddenly go away.

- Forgiveness doesn't mean always reconciling.

- That the abuser recognizes and owns his sin.

- We have not been wounded in relationships.

- Denying it ever happened. It may very well mean that we might have to change.

<u>*Forgiveness does mean ....*</u>

- God does not want us to be emotionally tormented, which results in lack of hope and joy.

- Nothing I can do to punish them will ever heal us / me.

- I "choose" not to dwell on it.

- I must "choose" to let it go and let God deal with the person who caused deep pain.

- Sometimes God allows us to walk through hurt and be wounded as He experienced on the cross.

- God works through our wounds to teach us authentic intimacy, grace and love.

- We never know the type of wine we are becoming when we are being crushed like grapes.

- God often times uses "misery" to build "ministry" opportunities to help others.

Food for thought ….

- Why do we avoid facing our wounds?

- We grieve God when we don't allow wholeness to happen. God wants to clean out every room of our home. The files and thoughts in our mind and the closets where we live.

- Honesty with self – Psalm 42:5   Agony is spiritual revitalization.

- Honesty with God – Psalm 62:8

- Honesty with safe people – Ecclesiastes 4:9-10

- Courage to forgive – Ephesians 4:31-32

- Learn to let go – Let it out. If you keep it inside, you only keep yourself in jail and hurt yourself.

- Give yourself permission to grieve – Ecclesiastes 3:4 – Death of a dream.

- Grief does not have to be a permanent address.

- If God were to write a letter to you about this stage of your life – what would he say?

❖ *The Purpose Driven Woman* … *Observe how she lived and learn from her actions*

- Abigail – I Samuel 25 – Looked out for her family

- Ruth – Loyal

- Both lost their husbands

- Acts of Kindness – God provided husband

- Wisdom, humble, courage, selflessness honorable motive, action – proactive, faithful, committed to her family, servants heart, women of strength, loyal, beautiful inside & out, respectful

- Communication that edified trust in God

- Learn to be content amidst your circumstances – Philippians 4:11-13

- Isaiah 40:27-29

- Relationship with Christ, Fruit of the Spirit, formed over time by thousands of wise choices – Proverbs 23:12

- Make a request, not a demand: "Could you …" or … "Would you …"

    - ✓ "I felt frustrated when you didn't take out the trash."
    - ✓ "I was really hurt when …" or "I really love the way you …"

- Inspiring words, meaningful touch, profitable time together, acts of kindness

- Making Peace with your Past

- Song of Solomon 2:7   Do not awaken love until it so desires

- We should not be ashamed to discuss what God created.
- Above all else, guard your heart, for it is the wellspring of life … Proverbs 4:23

- I will seek intimacy with God each day

- Sexual Purity

- Purpose (decide/choose) to be part of God's plan

- Seek healing and friendship

- Live life one day at a time

- Relationships take work, love, caring, effort

Remember …. The cause of an emotional disconnect can be due to lack of forgiveness and you will live in a self-made prison all your life. Forgiveness is a gift you give yourself and the other person.

❖ *<u>Homeopathic Doctors … Viva La Difference!</u>*

- Please know that if I ever break my leg or need a heart by-pass, I know that a hospital is the best place for these operations.

- However, have you ever considered visiting a doctor that believes that there are natural God given products that produce healing effects without the side effects of drugs? Do yourself a favor and Google homeopathy. Put your concern in the search bar and see what you discover.

- Remember, the FDA doesn't make any money if you don't buy their products, so they are not going to tell you about the vast array of natural products available at your health food store and about the doctors who know how to diagnose and treat your diseases with natural herbs that have no side effects!

- When I was 7 months pregnant with our son, I got a very bad hacking cough. It was extremely loud and painful to cough so hard. My pediatrician gave me cough medicine with codeine. Out of desperation I took it as prescribed. When the bottle was empty I called them and told them I was not any better than before I took it! They said the baby was draining my immune system and it was the only thing they could give me, and ordered another bottle. I had now been coughing for over a month!

Thankfully, that was the same week Alyson taught me about the word "Homeopathy" and I called the doctor she recommended. He assured me he could help and asked me to please not take any more of the cough medicine with codeine. I drove an hour to see him. Dr. Robert Jenkins listened to my lungs and gave me 2 bottles of herbs. I was to put 15 drops of each in a glass of water 3 times per day and call him in 3 days. Dr. Jenkins said I would be 90% better. Truly, I thought either you are wonderful ... or you have rocks in your belfry! I called Dr. Jenkins 3 days later and thanked him that I truly was 90% better. I was honestly amazed, as you may be, but have continued to see him for various issues and have been more than pleased with the results!!!

- What herbs were in this combination that was so effective you ask ... Echinacea Angust, Thuja Occident, and Myrrha. Thank the Lord for alternative medicine and the doctors who study it!!! Hum, think about it ... where have you heard the word myrrh before? Hint ... Remember the gifts brought to Jesus by the 3 Wise Men? They brought gold, frankincense and myrrh to the King of Kings in Bethlehem.

- When our son was just a year old, he had one ear infection after another and many rounds of antibiotics. Finally they sent us to see the surgeon to discuss putting tubes in Josh's ears. That same day I called Dr. Jenkins to get his opinion. He asked me to please bring Josh to see him and hold off on surgery. He gave us a bottle of Mullein Essence and I was to put drops in Josh's ears for 2 weeks and call him. I did and let him know that Josh seemed fine with no indication of any ear aches. He had me repeat this process for 2 more weeks and said Josh would never have another ear ache. I called him after the second 2 weeks and am happy to report that Josh never had another ear infection! That is true to this day and he is now 23 years old!

- One day I noticed that my toenail was getting thick and discolored. I went to the local doctor and he said it was a fungus; my toenail might fall off and never grow back. I was a bit taken back and said, "Is that the best you can do?" He assured me that was his diagnosis. I got home and called Dr. Jenkins who sent me a bottle of Tea Tree Oil. I applied it to my toe twice a day for 2 weeks and my toe nail is back to normal.

- Caution ... sometimes the products you can buy in the health food store are not as strong as those prescribed by homeopathic doctors, so you may want to check the correct potency with your homeopathic doctor and possibly order through his resources.

❖ *<u>Studies on the Mangosteen Fruit ... Possibly Just What Your Body Needs!</u>*

"Mangosteen – Known as the "Queen of Fruits"

Josh McDowell wrote the book, "**Evidence that Demands a Verdict**." Though some people try to disclaim God's word, the evidence is clear and demands a verdict. Likewise, though some people try to disclaim the research by National Institutes of Health and years of use and proof of amazing results found in using the mangosteen fruit, it is to your benefit to do your own research as every day is a gift and your health is worth fighting for every day! Is your health worth some research? Knowledge is power.

Mangosteen is one of the most highly regarded tropical fruits in Asia. Fondly known by Asians as the "Queen of Fruits," the exotic Mangosteen fruit is famous for being both exquisitely luscious and delicious and for its nutritional value. The mangosteen has been used for centuries in traditional medicine throughout the world and there are three decades of scientific laboratory studies to support its use.

In the scientific community, it is called **Garcinia Mangostana L**. In Vietnam, Mangosteen is called **cay mang cut**. It's **manggis** in Indonesia and Malaysia, **mongkhut** in Cambodia, **mangkhud** in Laos, and **mangkhut** in Thailand. In the Philippines, it's called **mangis** or **manggustan**.

J. Frederic Templeman, M.D. states that "Mangosteen is the gift your body deserves." The mangosteen fruit has been used for centuries in Southeast Asia and other tropical areas for numerous health applications. Traditional healers in Thailand, Cambodia, the Philippines, and India have utilized the fruit, the juice and the pericarp with very positive results.

Modern scientists have recently begun focusing on the value of the phytonutrients in mangosteen, and many have pointed to the fruit's impressive xanthone content as the major nutritional component deserving investigation.

Mangosteen also contains catechins. Catechins are a specialized group of flavonoids commonly found in plant species, most notably in tea plants. As flavonoids, they carry nutritional properties.

Proanthocyanidins are yet another class of phytonutrients found in the mangosteen. Research on this class of polyphenols is also impressive. Proanthocyanidins are antioxidant flavonoids that help in the stabilization of collagen and elastin – two critical proteins in the connective tissues that support organs, joints, blood vessels and muscle. Proanthocyanidins have been shown to support vascular health.

Truth will be better served if we all remember that the mangosteen is a food and act accordingly. To know exactly how your body will use the mangosteen nutrients requires personal experimentation.

__Further Research and Information: Take a minute to check out these links and learn even more about the power of xanthones and mangosteen.__

- Pubmed is a service of the US National Library of Medicine that includes over 19 million citations from MEDLINE and other life science journals. Colleges use this resource to teach their students about medical studies, and I encourage you to do some of your own research at *www.pubmed.org* by putting mangosteen and _____(your disorder) in the search bar to see what you discover. Then, forward this information to others you know would be interested in these topics. You may also search this site for mangosteen and xanthones – keys in the fight against free radicals.

- Video presentations at *"Life as it Could Be"* ... *www.lifeasitcouldbe.com*

- My website *www.sonshine.mymangosteen.com* will also give you further knowledge on this great tasting fruit. Experience the joy of being part of something bigger than yourself. ☺ Here's to your health!!! *

* Note: This information is for educational purposes only and should not be used to diagnose and treat diseases. All serious health conditions should be treated by a competent health practitioner. Neither the publisher nor the author in any way dispense medical advice, prescribe remedies, or assume responsibility for those who choose to treat themselves.

Two good friends and business associates of mine, Mark Bonner and Bill Shotwell are well versed on the benefits of the mangosteen fruit. You may contact Mark directly at: *my57mab@aol.com* or 703 / 791-3959.

Here is a personal note from Bill.

As a nutritional and holistic health counselor, I am not allowed by law to make any claims of what any natural foods or supplements will do or not do. However, I can tell you from personal experience that I have seen and heard first hand of many great and wonderful results. I can only speak for myself and my immediate family. This has changed our lives and has truly amazing results. This is some compelling information. Do yourself a big favor and take a look at this.

Mangosteen is a food, not a chemical or drug.

If there is the slightest chance that this all natural fruit from the orient could be beneficial to you, why would you not try it?

If you are interested in an "overview" that you can view on your computer, just send me your contact information and I will register you to view a short (25 to 35 minute) Internet presentation LIVE from the comfort of your home.

You will be in my prayers. Please do not hesitate to call if I can be of any assistance. Be well.

Believe!

Bill Shotwell   shotwellw@yahoo.com   703 / 675 3537

I am only a phone call away.

Chapter 15

✓ ***Excellent Books to Read, DVD & Video Series, and Some of My Favorite Songs***

✓ **Attitude, Perspective, Perseverance, Success**

- *The Greatest Miracle in the World* … by Og Mendino. Yes, you are **the greatest miracle in the world**! Maybe you don't think of yourself as a **miracle**. Maybe you take yourself for granted. …

- *How to Win Friends & Influence People* … by Dale Carnegie. One of the first bestselling self-help books ever published.

- *Surrendered Christian Athlete* … by Brant C. Tolsma. What would happen to a gifted athlete if he trained his heart with the same dedication as he trained his body? "Christ in you, the hope of glory" is his theme. "Run to win" is his motivation. "Play for Him" is his audience.

- *The Magic of Thinking Big* … by Dr. David J. Schwartz. Useful methods, not empty promises.

- *The 7 Habits of Highly Effective People* ... Stephen R. Covey. Learn the difference between the philosophy referred to as the Personality Ethic and the Character Ethic where success is attributed more to underlying characteristics such as integrity, courage, justice, patience, etc. Ralph Waldo Emerson once said, "What you are shouts so loudly in my ears I cannot hear what you say." The author presents an "inside-out" approach to effectiveness that is centered on principles and character. For many people, this approach represents a paradigm shift.

- *Rich Dad Poor Dad* ... by Richard Kiyasoki. In reading *Rich Dad Poor Dad*, you'll better understand the power that thinking can have on your life. If you are looking for financial freedom, then *Rich Dad Poor Dad* is a great place to start your learning process.

- *Think & Grow Rich* ... by Napoleon Hill. "Truly, thoughts are things – and powerful things at that when they are mixed with definiteness of purpose, persistence, and a burning desire that translates into actions.

- *Tempered Steel* ... by Steve Farrar. Making steel is no walk in the park. The process requires unbelievable heat and searing fire. But what you have at the end is very, very strong and yet can be shaped by a master's hands. In the Psalms we see God's man David endure crushing pressure and fiery trials and emerge on the other side, shaped by the hand of God for greatness. In today's uncertain world men still face the stress and heat of adversity. But God can use that fire in a man's life and bring him through it all – strong, purified, flexible, and ready for anything.

- *Has Christianity Failed You?* **DVD Series by Ravi Zacharias and Michael Ramsden**

The barriers to belief in the Christian gospel often reach far beyond the intellect as we search for truth and meaning in a fallen world. Too many people have been disappointed or hurt by the church and/or individual Christians -- and then, have turned away from Christianity, harboring deep-seated feelings of distrust and bitterness.

On May 11, 2006, Ravi Zacharias and Michael Ramsden, before a sold-out audience at Atlanta's renowned Fox Theatre, tackled the seeming failure of Christianity to respond with relevance and compassion in real-world experiences.

"That's how it has failed us – when it becomes part of the judgment that divides us rather than the Grace that unites us."

Disc One replays that dramatic evening, with both messages, plus a 35 minute Q&A session in which some of the most difficult personal conflicts were voiced by earnest seekers. On Disc Two, Ravi and Michael continue to respond to those questions that could not be addressed during the evening because of time constraints; as well as other bonus features. This set is jam-packed with content!

- *Turn Setbacks into Greenbacks: 7 Secrets for Going Up in Down Times* … by Willie Jolley is a self-empowerment guide to help you find victory from the jaws of defeat. It is a powerful, timely survival guide that will teach you how to survive while others are failing. It will help you develop the mind-set to succeed. Just as a caterpillar must struggle to force his body out of the cocoon which strengthen its wings for flight, we must also understand that "Your set-back is a set-up for a come-back!"

✓ **Communication**

- *Love & Respect* … Emerson Eggerichs is a "light bulb moment!" Actually, I would highly recommend his DVD as he is so animated that you will laugh and laugh, but he is also very good at painting word pictures that "solve the whole communication mystery between men and women." It is truly worth your time and the light bulb will go on in your understanding and others will seek you out for advice! The workbook is well designed for quick review in time of need!

- *The Five Love Languages* … How to Express Heartfelt Commitment to Your Mate by Gary Chapman. Have you ever tried to do something you thought another would enjoy only to find out they are not pleased with your gift? Understand why by understanding that their love language just might be different and might express itself differently than yours!

- *The DNA of Relationships* ... Discover how you are designed for satisfying relationships by Dr. Gary Smalley. Relationships are like a dance step and this one has a unique approach to explain how God designed us, how to resolve conflict and experience an increase in relationship satisfaction.

- *The Language of Love* ... A powerful way to maximize insight, intimacy, and understanding by Gary Smalley & John Trent, Ph.D., authors of The Two Sides of Love.

- *To a Child LOVE is Spelled T-I-M-E* ... by MacAnderson and Lance Wubbels. These men remind us that our time is our most precious gift. A hundred years from now will it really matter what your bank account looked like on a given day, if all the repairs were done on the house, or the kind of car you drove? However, the world may be different because you were important in the life of a child. To the world you may be just one person, but to that one person you may be their world.

- *The Power of a Praying Parent* ... Stormie Omartian. Award-winning author, singer, and songwriter Stormie Omartian and her husband, Michael, spent 20 years raising their children ... and learning the power of praying for them. Learn how you can pray through each stage of your child's growth, from early childhood through adulthood, turning to the Father and placing every detail of your child's life in His loving and capable hands.

- *For Women Only* ... Shaunti Feldhahn. Understand the heart of your man. What Shaunti Feldhahn's research reveals about the inner lives of men will open women's eyes to what the men in their life – boyfriends, brothers, husbands, and sons - are really thinking and feeling. Men want to be understood, but they're afraid to "freak out" the women they love by confessing what is happening inside their heads.

- *For Men Only* … by Shaunti Feldhahn. Understand the heart of your woman. Finally, You Can Understand Her! Women: complicated and impossible to understand? The bestselling author of *For Women Only* teams with her husband to offer men the key to unlocking the mysterious ways of women. Through Shaunti and Jeff Feldhahn's national scientific survey and hundreds of interviews, *For Men Only* reveals what you can do today to improve your relationship. What makes her tick? What is she really asking (but not actually saying)? Take the guesswork out of trying to please your wife or girlfriend and begin loving her in the way she needs. Easily. *For Men Only* is a straightforward map that will lead you straight into her heart.

✓ **Life Issues**

- *Who Moved My Cheese* … Spencer Johnson, MD. I found this little book very helpful when I was mentally and emotionally stuck at a point in my life and couldn't seem to find my way out of a wet paper bag!

- *The Ultimate Gift* … by Jim Stovall comes as a book and DVD and is well worth the watching and reading. What really matters in helping a young person learn the values of life that will sustain him/her throughout their lifetime? This is a cleaver way to instill those values and see results. An enjoyable read with a heartwarming story. Each day, the momentum grows and the impact widens, as The Ultimate Gift continues to inspire millions to share the gift and change the world.

- *Wild At Heart … for Men* … A great book and DVD series by John Eldredge helps men understand the warrior and sense of adventure that indwells guys from the time they are little. It helps us mom's understand why everything and anything becomes a gun or weapon to help fight off the bad guys. Little boys are built for adventure … it's in the DNA! The Wild At Heart DVD and audio series is also available and will minister to the heart of men.

- *<u>Captivating ... for Women</u>* ... A woman has very different DNA than a man and from the time she is a small child dressing up and looking in the mirror helps us get a glimpse into her heart's longing to be in a relationship, to be wanted, to be beautiful, to be captivating. John & Stasi Eldredge wrote this book to help you get a glimpse of her heart and the question she wants you to answer.

- *<u>The New Evidence that Demands a Verdict</u>* ... Josh McDowell gives in-depth historical evidences for the Christian Faith, updated to answer the questions challenging Christians today. As a young man, Josh McDowell considered himself an agnostic. He truly believed that Christianity was worthless. However, when challenged to intellectually examine the claims of Christianity, Josh discovered compelling, overwhelming evidence for the reliability of the Christian faith. After trusting in Jesus Christ as Savior and Lord, Josh's life changed dramatically as he experienced the power of God's love.

    Well known as an articulate speaker, Josh has addressed more than 10 million young people, giving over 24,000 talks in 118 countries. Josh is a Christian apologist, evangelist, and writer. He is the author or co-author of some 77 books.

- *<u>Defining Moments - When Choices Matter Most</u>* ...by Dan Schaefer. Life decisions can make or break you. You can be prepared to do the right thing when those defining moments take you by surprise.

    Pastor Dan Schaeffer reminds you, "One morning you wake up, totally unaware that today you will make a decision that will define your life for years to come, perhaps forever. If you had known this moment was approaching, you would have prepared for it. But you didn't . . . That moment is coming—maybe today, perhaps in a week, a month, or a year, but it is coming, and you won't be able to escape it . . . You can hope you will say or do the right thing, or you can prepare for that moment now."

    <u>Defining Moments</u> highlights the lives of real people in real-life situations to encourage you and prepare you for your own life defining moments.

- *Home is Where Life Makes Up Its Mind* ... by Charles R. Swindoll. Life happens in your home on a daily basis and your toddler is watching you! How you live your life and how you train and teach them as toddlers will be very telling when they are 15 and older.

- *The One Year Book of Devotions for Kids* – Best-Selling Series. Each book offers 365 Character-Building Principles by Tyndale House Publishers, Inc. A great way to discuss today's hot issues through a collection of fun-filled and spiritually enriching stories designed just for kids. Set aside a time after dinner when the whole family is present to read these one-page stories and let the discussion begin!

- *Logged On and Tuned Out* ... Vicki Courtney writes a timely wake-up call to low-tech (tuned out) parents whose high-tech (logged on) kids use modern computer and cell phone technology like second nature. In simple language, moms and dads overwhelmed by today's digital world will learn the imperative basics and checkpoints of Instant Messaging, text messaging, social networking Web sites (MySpace, Facebook), chat rooms, and photo and video uploading. Learn that through technology your kids may easily be accessing information that will affect their future in a negative way. Focus on the Family reminds us to be on the offensive and the defensive with your kids. Open communication and put a filter on your computer that tells you where they have been and if they have stumbled on to any sites that would choose to lure them and suck them into negative input.

- *The New Dare to Discipline* ... by Dr. James Dobson of Focus on the Family. Self-control, human kindness, respect, and peacefulness can again be manifest in America if we will **dare to discipline** in our homes and schools. Children need love, trust, affection--and discipline. From one generation to the next, the challenge of helping to nurture children into becoming responsible adults doesn't change. Dr. Dobson's classic *Dare to Discipline,* a practical, reassuring guide for caring parents, has sold over 2 million copies since its release in 1970. What gives a book that kind of staying power? The ability to meet a real, felt need in the marketplace. Today, a whole new generation of parents is turning to Dr. Dobson's wise counsel. Some things never change.

- *The Total Transformation Program* created by behavioral therapist James Lehman. Do you struggle with your child's behavior? Do the research and find out the cause, the solution and how to make tomorrow different from today. This program gives you direct access to the Parent Support Line where you can get answers "in the moment" for your crisis situation. For more information call 800 / 711-4108. http://www.thetotaltransformation.com

- *Have a New Kid by Friday* … child psychologist, Dr. Kevin Leman, gives humorous, insightful and effective advice on many behavioral problems for every childhood age and stage. If potty training is driving you crazy, he's got it covered. If you need help teaching your kids to become more respectful of one another, he can help. And if you want to prevent your teens from lighting up, Dr. Leman addresses that, too. Dr. Leman's gives expert advice on these and many other parenting challenges, including eating and under-eating challenges, wardrobe issues, tattling and put-downs. For further information visit:

  www.focusonthefamily.com/…/4_secrets_to_successfully_handling_behavior_problems.aspx

  And more results at:

  www.focusonthefamily.com/parenting/effective_biblical_discipline

  According to Leman, healthy self-esteem is cultivated in children through **A**cceptance, **B**elonging and **C**ompetence. His clever discipline method is less exhausting and more successful than ranting, raving, blaming, pleading, begging or threatening. Learn more at:

  www.focusonthefamily.com/…/why_kids_misbehave/building_selfesteem_in_your_kids.aspx

- *Hooked* … Drs. Freda Bush and Joe McIlhaney, experts on brain development and sexuality, discuss how the brain is related to sex, how casual sex is affecting our teens, and how to sow the seeds of abstinence:

You've heard it said that the brain is the most important sex organ. Drs. Freda Bush and Joe McIlhaney explain how science bears that out. These doctors also talk to parents about some of the consequences of premarital sex, including STDs, compulsive behavior, attachment disorders, and more. They encourage parents to love their teens, to remain involved in their lives, and let them know their standards regarding premarital sex. Freda tells what she and her husband's response was when their own daughter came home from college and announced she was pregnant.

Neuro-chemical changes occur in the brain and you are not the same after sexual intimacy. Learn about oxytosin and dopamine and the effects they have every time you are intimate. Learn about the link between sex and attachment. Having multiple partners is like putting tape on and off ... eventually it has no ability to stick. During acts of intimacy, changes occur in the brain and you are not the same.

Society tells us that sex is an act of self-expression, a personal choice for physical pleasure that can be summed up in the ubiquitous phrase "hooking up." Millions of American teenagers and young adults are finding that the psychological baggage of such behavior is having a real and lasting impact on their lives. They are discovering that "hooking up" is the easy part, but "unhooking" from the bonds of a sexual relationship can have serious consequences.

A practical look into new scientific research shows how sexual activity causes the release of brain chemicals which then result in emotional bonding and a powerful desire to repeat the activity. This book will help parents and singles understand that "safe sex" isn't safe at all; that even if they are protected against STDs and pregnancy, they are still hurting themselves and their partners.

- *Interviewing Your Daughter's Date* ... 8 Steps to No Regrets by Dennis Rainey, Host of Family Life Today. As a dad, you want to protect your daughter, especially from boys with super-charged hormones! Just the thought of it makes you break out into a cold sweat. Interviewing Your Daughter's Date will walk you through 8 principles that Dennis Rainey used to help his own daughters navigate through the dating years, with their emotions calm, their heart whole, and their character intact. You'll learn how to protect your daughter, set boundaries in her relationships, and give her guidance as she grows up. Matt McPoland's perspective is that it is a great book that hit's the point on the head ... the father needs to be involved and protect his daughter at all costs. I learned so much in so little time ... I keep going back to this resource because I have 4 daughters!

- ***College Ready: Making the Most of Your Next Great Adventure*** ... Robert Lewis and John Bryson can help you make the most of your college years. This six part high impact video series is designed to help you understand the college maze; recognize the key areas you will need to succeed in, and craft a plan and personal vision for starting college right and finishing it well. Don't let your students face it unprepared. Get them ready. Incoming students need to feel confident about the new experience that awaits them. You can equip them with this fast-paced, informative resource designed to help high school seniors and college freshmen think clearly, wisely, and strategically about the college years ahead. Prepare your students for the many changes, challenges, and opportunities that college will bring. *www.collegeready.com*

College Ready is a video-guided experience that addresses six important topics:

Dating Right	College Starts Best with Vision
Having Fun	Empowering Friendships
Growing Spiritually	Excelling Academically

- *The Purpose Driven Life* ... What on Earth am I here for? Rick Warren takes a look at knowing God's purpose for creating you which will reduce your stress, focus your energy, simplify your decisions, give meaning to your life and most important, prepare you for eternity. You are not an accident!

- *Tender Warrior: God's Intention for Man* ... by Stu Weber. King. Warrior. Mentor. Friend. Stu Weber paints a dramatic and compelling picture of balanced manhood according to God's blueprint. A Tender Warrior is what every woman dreams of for a husband, every boy desires to be, and every man yearns most to develop within himself. Written in a warm, personal style, Weber presents the characteristics of tender warriors, including watching out for what lies ahead, keeping commitments, and learning to speak the language of women, in an upfront, straightforward style that challenges readers to realize God's plan for men.

- *How to Get a Date Worth Keeping* … by Dr. Henry Cloud. Another Friday Night Alone is not what you are looking for and Dr. Cloud says you can put an end to the datelessness. Starting today – right now – you can begin a journey that will bring fun and interesting people into your life which will broaden your experience of others and yourself, and lead you toward the date of all dates – a date worth keeping.

- *Change Your Brain … Change Your Life* … by Daniel G. Amen. The Breakthrough Program for Conquering Anxiety, Depression, Obsessiveness, Anger, and Impulsiveness

- *The Total Money Makeover* … Dave Ramsey condenses his 17 years of financial teaching and counseling into **7 organized, easy-to-follow steps** that will lead you out of debt and into a Total Money Makeover. Plus, you'll read **over 50 real-life stories** from people just like you who have followed these principles and are **now winning with their money**. It is a plan **designed for everyone**, regardless of income or age. With *The Total Money Makeover*, you'll be able to:

  ✓ Design a sure-fire plan for paying off ALL debt
  ✓ Recognize the 10 most dangerous money myths
  ✓ Secure a big, fat nest egg for emergencies and retirement
  ✓ Positively change your life and your family tree!

- *Peacemaking for Families* … by Ken Sande, Tom Raabe. Bless your family by learning and implementing the valuable principles found in *Peacemaking for Families*: the Peacemaker's Pledge, the Seven A's of Forgiveness, and the PAUSE principle of negotiation. With the help of engaging real-life stories, you'll learn how to create a harmonious environment based on basic conflict resolution skills found in Scripture. A *Focus on the Family* resource.

- *DivorceCare Video Series* with 13 seminars that feature contemporary Christian authors and leaders who share insights and testimonies of God's mercy and grace. These dynamic videos also include personal testimonies from people who have been through divorce. The series will touch your heart, minister to your soul and help you heal. Many churches purchase the kit which includes the videos, workbooks with a note-taking outline for the video sessions, a daily Bible study and recommended books for further growth and healing. To locate a seminar/support group near you, go on-line and Google DivorceCare.

- *DivorceCare for Kids* will help minimize the effects of divorce on your children's schoolwork, emotional health and spiritual life. Children struggle deeply with separation and divorce. As they begin to heal from the pain and confusion, their relationships with you, God and others will grow healthy and strong. Hundreds of DC4K groups meet in Christian churches throughout the US, Canada and other countries. There is one meeting near you! Connect your children with a DC4K group today. *http://www.dc4k.org/parentzone/library/*

- *Epicenter* – **Why the Current Rumblings in the Middle East Will Change Your Future** ... Joel Rosenberg. In his first nonfiction book, this evangelical Christian from an Orthodox Jewish heritage takes readers on an unforgettable journey through prophecy and current events into the future of Iraq after Saddam, Russia after Communism, Israel after Arafat, and Christianity after radical Islam. You won't want to miss Joel's exclusive interviews with Israeli, Palestinian, and Russian leaders, and previously classified CIA and White House documents. Similar to the approach Joel takes in his novels, his desire is to draw readers into stories, anecdotes, and predictions in a way that builds confidence that allows Joel to share his faith in Jesus Christ and the reliability of Scripture as a guide to understanding the past and the future.

- *The Prayer of Jabez* … Bruce Wilkinson. What happens when ordinary Christians decide to reach for an extraordinary life – which, as it turns out, is exactly the kind God promises.

- *The Bucket List* … DVD featuring Jack Nicholson and Morgan Freeman. This is a comedy film that is heartwarming and thought provoking as it follows two terminally ill men on their road trip with a wish list of things to do before they "kick the bucket."

- *The Pursuit of Happyness* … Will Smith - DVD

✓ **Medical**

- *The Maker's Diet* … The 40-day health experience that will change your life forever by Jordan S. Rubin. Biblically based and scientifically proven. **The Maker's Diet** uses a truly holistic approach to health. This groundbreaking book leads you on a journey that will help you boost your immune system, attain and maintain your ideal weight, have abundant energy, reduce stress ….

- *Juicing For Life* … Cherie Calbom and Maureen Keane provide a guide to the health benefits of fresh fruit and vegetable juicing. Did you know that eating fresh fruits and vegetables can boost your energy level, supercharge your immune system, and maximize your body's healing power? The United States Surgeon General, the National Cancer Institute, Congress, the world's top scientists and medical researchers, and the most highly respected doctors and nutritionists all now endorse this approach to health.

- *4 Blood Types, 4 Diets … Eat Right 4 Your Type, Diet Solution to Staying Healthy, Living Longer and Achieving Your Ideal Weight* … Dr. Peter J. D'Adamo with Catherene Whitney. Did you know that **your Blood Type** makes a difference as to what foods your body craves! Who would have ever guessed? Check it out. Would you believe our dietary needs are as unique as our fingerprints! We are biochemical individuals and Dr. D'Adamo gives practical ways to apply this information to our lives. He explains that the secret to healthy disease-free living might be as simple as knowing your blood type!

- *<u>The Best Kept Secrets to Healthy Aging</u>* ... Barry S. Kendler PhD, FACN, CNS. Your Guide to Better Health and Longevity by The Purity Research Department. Advanced nutritional strategies for better health and longevity with hundreds of scientific footnotes.

- *<u>SuperFoods Rx</u>* ... Steven Pratt, M.D., witnessed the positive results that occurred when his patients with age-related macular degeneration changed their diets to include certain powerhouse foods – those he has identified as SuperFoods. Backed by proven research on fourteen of the most nutrient-dense foods, this book puts these tools in your hands, and on your plate, to give you more energy, greater protection against disease and a healthy lifestyle now and for the future.

- *<u>What You Don't Know May Be Killing YOU!</u>* ... Don Colbert, M.D., is board-certified in family practice and specializes in nutritional therapies.

- *<u>Prescription for Nutritional Healing</u>* ... James F & Phyllis A. Balch. Have you ever wished someone had figured out what herbs to take that would help various conditions? For many years people interested in alternative healing and preventative therapies have relied on this invaluable reference as a guide to improve health through nutrition and supplementation, avoiding traditional drug therapies.

- *<u>Healing ADD – ADHD</u>* ... Dr. Daniel Amen. Research studies have been done on the brain to see how it functions, what transpires when medication is given, and pictures are presented in the book for you to see the results for yourself. <u>www.amenclinic.com</u>

- *<u>Homeopathy Medicine that Works!</u>* ... Exciting new hope for suffers of every kind. Robert S. Wood shares the discovery of what safe holistic medicine can do for you. Homeopathic physicians can cure chronic allergies, arthritis, asthma, gout, heart disease, hypertension, depression, schizophrenia, psychological afflictions, hereditary disorders, infectious diseases, skin conditions, major injuries, and deep chronic afflictions of every kind – even early stage cancer and AIDS.

- *Let's Get Well* ... Adelle Davis was a pioneer and visionary in the field of nutrition. Her books are essential reading for anyone interested in the history of nutrition and healthful eating.

- *Fit for Life* ... Nutrition specialists Harvey and Marilyn Diamond explain how you can eat more kinds of food than you ever ate before without counting calories ... and still lose weight! The natural body cycle, permanent weight-loss plan that proves it's not only what you eat, but also when and how.

- *Healthy Aging* ... Barry S. Kendler, PhD, FACN, CNS. Your guide to Better Health and Longevity. Cutting-edge secrets on how to enhance your energy levels, improve your physical appearance, invigorate your sex drive, and promote overall physical, cognitive and emotional health to live life to its fullest.

✓ *Some of My Favorite Songs*

Open your web-browser and enjoy viewing and listening to these on **www.youtube.com**

- *Find Your Wings … Mark Harris …* Great song from parent to child
  http://www.youtube.com/watch?v=-4NS7gChzvk

- *Watching You … Rodney Atkins …* Great reminder that kids repeat what they see and look up to you for the right example!
  http://www.youtube.com/watch?v=oqYUns2YQik

- *Majesty … Worship His Majesty …*
  http://www.youtube.com/watch?v=OaRwD2Y7C0s

- *Complete … Parachute Band …*
  http://www.youtube.com/watch?v=rNYc5El60PI&feature

- *God Must Have Spent a Little More Time on You … Nsync*
  http://www.youtube.com/watch?v=-fxh7jAJR8U

- *I Loved Her First … Heartland …* Great dance music for father and bride.
  http://www.youtube.com/watch?v=sH3rPYMUfEQ

- *You Raise Me Up … Josh Groban …*
  http://www.youtube.com/watch?v=EYFC4god3lo&feature

- *Worthy is the Lamb … The Brooklyn Tabernacle Choir …*
  http://www.youtube.com/watch?v=4Gae-n0Pb7Q

- *The Touch of the Master's Hand … 1Naphi*
  http://www.youtube.com/watch?v=qoBueoUnrIY

- *I Will Never Be the Same Again* … Hillsong …
  http://www.youtube.com/watch?v=yptnKmsVmgo

- *I've Just Seen Jesus* … Sandi Patti & Larnelle Harris …
  http://www.youtube.com/watch?v=PLGTXz-txTY

- *Potter's Hand* … Darlene Zschech (Hillsong) …
  http://www.youtube.com/watch?v=xDAITgJXO1I

- *Eagles Wings* … Hillsong …
  http://www.youtube.com/watch?v=YNiJZIs_tgk

- *Don't Save It All For Christmas Day* … Avalon
  http://www.youtube.com/watch?v=ki4EOL0Ihf0&feature=related

- *Here I am Lord* … Steve Silvia …
  http://www.youtube.com/watch?v=otaSC_NHlCw

- *Alabaster Box* … CeCe Winans
  http://www.youtube.com/watch?v=s9QZxS03FvY&feature=related

- *More Than Wonderful* … Sandi Patti & Larnelle Harris …
  http://www.youtube.com/watch?v=6CcebZCl_DM

- *All For the Glory of You* … Mark Harris …
  http://www.youtube.com/watch?v=q-6aeJ8sqLA

- *On Eagle's Wings* … mhcaillesrn
  http://www.youtube.com/watch?v=4rRea9qnjK4

- *Come and Fill My Heart* … Avalon
  http://www.youtube.com/watch?v=7E7no65TotM&feature=related

- *Salt & Light … Jamie Smith*
  http://www.youtube.com/watch?v=Cd_gnvnAV8U&feature=related

- *I'm Amazed … Jason Crab*
  http://www.youtube.com/watch?v=VJWLGLtRXXk&feature=related

- *I Can Only Imagine … Mercy Me*
  http://www.youtube.com/watch?v=Lv3mOPCH6bs

- *Sometimes He Calms the Storm … Scott Krippayne*
  http://www.youtube.com/watch?v=9Ti1SULYteI

Who Am I
imation
CD-RW | 1x-4x
700MB, 80 min
Through His Eyes
His thoughts
are not our own.
Am7
just
a man;
G/B
Am7/D
un - der - stand,
G
G/B
Am7
G

Appendix ... Lots of Helpful Questionnaires and Other Items for You!

Questions to Ask During Phone Interview for Job Opportunity ...

- Make sure you know the name of the company and the person you are speaking with:

    Contact: _____ Phone #: _____
    Company Name: _____

    Company Website ... so you can look at it: _____

- Where are you located: (You have to drive the miles every day soooo you want to know.) _____

- Approximate number of people in the company: _____
  # working at this location? _____

- Personalities of the people you will be working with: _____

- Ask them to e-mail you the job description. Then you can review it!

- As you see it, what will be my toughest challenge in this position? _____
  _____

- If you like what you hear, tell them: I think I would be a very good candidate for this position.

Job Pointers ... Things to Remember

- You only get one chance to make a "Good First Impression." Dress for success and look your best.

- If finances are a challenge for you at this time and you don't have clothes you feel are appropriate for an interview, visit your local thrift shop and be amazed what people give away!!!

- From the list of "Interview Questions" pick the questions that best suit this interview.

- Go with a positive attitude.

- Sit forward and look interested.

- Remember to smile. Take a deep breath and try to look interested and relaxed.

- Greet people with a positive solid (but not wrenching) hand shake. Remember in your enthusiasm not to squeeze a woman's hand too tight as you can cause pain on her smaller fingers ... especially if she is wearing rings!

- Remember - First impressions count! Look your best and don't forget to introduce yourself to the receptionist, ask her name and smile. When you sit down and are waiting for your interview, write down her name so you can greet her by name when you come back for your 2nd interview! She may have input on weather or not you get the job.

Interview Questionnaire

Phone #: _____

Company: _____ Spoke with: _____ Date: _____

Location: _____ Start Date: _____

1. Describe this position as you see it. (Describe a normal day or work week.)
   _____
   _____

   Atmosphere: _____

2. What are your immediate goals & priorities for this position? _____
   _____
   _____

3. What are going to be the biggest challenges I would have in this position? _____
   _____

4. What characteristics best describe individuals who are successful in this position? How would you describe the ideal candidate for this position? _____
   _____

5. Opportunities for growth? _____

6. How I see my background, work experience, etc. are a match. What I can offer your Company. Tell them what they said they needed. Match individual skills to job requirements. Show how I can fill the need.

7. <u>Attributes:</u> Enjoy a challenge, take initiative, goal oriented, team player, strong interpersonal skills, drive & determination to bring project to completion.

8. How would you describe the organization's culture / environment? _____
   _____

9. What makes your organization different from the competition? _____
   _____

10. I would like the opportunity to fill the position. Do you consider me a strong candidate for this position? _____

11. Salary: That's a good question! What are you prepared to pay your best candidate?
    _____

    Commissions: _____ Bonus: _____

12. Start contributing to 401K after _____ months. # Weeks Vacation: _____
    # of Holidays: _____ Stock Options: _____

    Week - Christmas & New Year's:
    Hours: _____ Overtime: _____ Travel: _____ Credit Union: _____
    Vesting: _____ Medical: _____ Dental: _____
    Ask for Business Card: _____

❖ When it is time for my review and you are extremely happy ... What have I done?
  _____

How to Choose A Credit Card that's Right for YOU!

You know yourself better than anyone else. First, Decide How YOU will use your credit card.

A. Will you PAY OFF Your Balance Every Month? Circle one choice: YES   NO

B. Will you have a Balance and need to Pay INTEREST on Your Balance? In this case, make sure the credit card you choose offers a VERY LOW INTEREST RATE. Credit Card Interest Rate: _____%. It is EXTREMELY IMPORTANT to understand this step. If not, INTEREST that accrues on a monthly basis will begin to EAT YOU UP and it is then hard to catch up and pay off YOUR bill. This occurs because you are buying more things than you can afford. If this is you, than maybe FREE Frequent Flyer Miles through the use of a credit card is NOT a good option for you. Be honest with yourself.

However, if you are or can be disciplined enough to carry your checkbook or a tablet with you along with your credit card and WRITE DOWN every purchase, i.e. the date of your purchase, put CC for Credit Card in the space for your check number (as you didn't actually write a check for your purchase), the name of the store and the amount spent in your checkbook. Then subtract the amount of your purchase from your balance so that you know your correct total amount of cash available. This is very important so you are not spending more money than what your balance says you have in your checkbook. At the end of the month you will receive a statement from your credit card company and you can just write one check to cover all the items you have purchased.

C. If you are interested in FREE Frequent Flyer Miles, the next step is to decide where you might like to fly and what airlines travel to those destinations. Then choose a credit card that gives you frequent flyer miles on airlines that fly where you want to go. <u>Note:</u> **It is best to choose one credit card and put all your purchases on this one card so that all your FREE Frequent Flyer Miles are in one account. You cannot usually transfer frequent flyer miles from one credit** card account to another, unless they are with the same credit card company. I recommend a credit card that lets you fly on "Any Airline."

D. Make sure that the credit card you choose awards you at least **1 FREE Frequent Flyer Mile for every $ you spend. Occasionally you will find those that offer 2 and 3 Frequent Flyer Miles for every $ spent.**

E. When you call a credit card company be sure to ask how many frequent flyer miles it takes to fly to your destination. Usually it takes 20,000-25,000 frequent flyer miles to fly anywhere in the Continental United States and 30,000 to 35,000 to fly outside the 48 Continental US states. Air travel to Europe and the islands is usually 45,000 Frequent Flyer Miles. There are some credit card companies that only require 16,000 points/miles to fly across the US using a formula of the cost of the ticket you find on-line x 80 to give you the number of Frequent Flyer Miles you will need. (Example: If the ticket costs $200 x 80 = 16,000 Frequent Flyer Miles)

F. Check the **ANNUAL FEE** for each credit card you are considering.

$_____ Visa $_____ Master Card $_____ American Express

G. Note: Some credit cards offer Frequent Flyer Miles for only one airline, and others offer fights on several, and some on any airline. So check it out and determine the following:

I want to fly to: _____

Airlines that Fly to this destination: _____, _____, _____

Questions to Ask and Information to Note from Credit Card Companies Offering FREE Frequent Flyer Miles

Some of this information you can pull from their websites and you may want to call them to clarify the information. Start your research on-line and look up: Frequent Flyer Miles.

Date: _____ Contact Name: _____

Type of Credit Card: _____ Visa _____ Master Card

I do not recommend American Express as there is a $75 annual fee to have an American Express card and you cannot use it at all locations.

Issuing Company (Bank): _____ Phone #: _____

1. Does each dollar in purchases equal 1, 2 or 3 **Frequent Flyer Miles**?   Yes   No

2. Do you offer a card that gives me **Double or Triple Frequent Flyer Miles** for each dollar I spend?   Yes   No

3. Does each dollar in purchases equal 1 or More **Bonus Points** good for items other than Frequent Flyer Miles?   Yes   No

4. Which airlines can I fly with this card? _____

5. Are there any Restrictions on Booking my Flights?

APPENDIX ... LOTS OF HELPFUL QUESTIONNAIRES AND OTHER ITEMS FOR YOU! ▪ 201

- Black Out Dates (Days when you *cannot fly* under this program – like holidays): _____

- Is a 21 Day Advance Purchase Required? _____
- Is a Saturday Night stay Required? _____

6. When I want to make my airline reservations, do I:

    - Just call an 800 number and select and book my flights over the phone?
    - Or do I check on-line for the best available flights, book them myself, and then call within 90 days to redeem my miles and credit my account for the cost of the airline ticket?

7. Which airlines can I fly with this card? _____

8. Any Restrictions on Booking my Flights?

    - Black Out Dates (Days when you *cannot fly* under this program – like holidays): _____

    - Is a 21 Day Advance Purchase Required? _____
    - Is a Saturday Night stay Required? _____

9. Can I fly in the US, Bermuda, Bahamas, Hawaii, Europe? (Where do you want to fly?) _____

    - How many FF Miles does it take to fly anywhere in the United States: _____

    - How many FF Miles will I need to fly outside the US: _____
    - How many FF Miles will I need to fly (where ever you want to go!) _____

10. Can I use my Frequent Flyer Miles to purchase airline tickets for someone else? _____

202 ▪ NOW THAT'S A GREAT IDEA!

11. If I use my Frequent Flyer Miles to purchase an airline ticket and find I need to cancel the trip, can I change the date and destination? _____
   _____

   - What is the cost to change the date? $ _____
   - Can I use the same ticket to fly to a different destination? _____

12. What other ways can I use my ***FREE Frequent Flyer Miles***? Can I use them for hotel stays, a rental car, a cruise weekend get-away, beach property?

13. Do Frequent Flyer Miles Expire? _____ How many years are they good for? _____

   a. As long as I "book a trip" before my miles expire, is it true that I can actually fly after the expiration date? _____

14. What is the cost to use your credit card during the 1st year: $ _____
   What is the cost for Additional Years? $ _____

   Cost: $ _____ for Credit Limit to $ _____ ...
   Cost: $ _____ for Credit Limit to $ _____

15. INTEREST that accrues if I do not pay my bill **In Full** each month? _____%
   1st Year: _____% 2nd Year: _____% Additional Years: _____%

16. Can I pay my mortgage or college expenses on this credit card and accrue Frequent Flyer Miles for these expenses? Yes   No

17. Do you offer a Sign-Up Bonus? _____ If Yes, # of miles gained after initial purchase: _____ Bonus Miles.

18. Do you offer a Referral Bonus? _____ If Yes, # of miles gained after initial approval: _____.

For those of you who like to do research, here is a website authored by Gary Steiger that I discovered and you may find interesting as part of your research.

http://www.freefrequentflyermiles.com/index.htm

Renting A Room in Your Home

- Check prices listed in your area and post your notice on your local church website, bulletin board, etc.
- Do a "Phone Interview" to determine if they sound like a good candidate
- Set a day and time and Invite them over for an "In-Person Interview"
- Housing Agreement
- Housing Etiquette … It takes "team effort" to make a house feel like a home!
- Items to Remember as you are Planning to Move on to the Next Chapter of Your Life…
- Eviction Notice … I hope you never need to use this one!

Ladies - Rooms Available in (Your City)

Ladies – Rooms Available in Clarkstown - In a lovely setting on 2/3 of an acre, I currently have two rooms off the family room of my home awaiting your arrival. I'm a Christian woman who attends _____ Bible Church and I rent two rooms in my home. Use of kitchen, laundry room, dining room, deck and the swing and hammock by the old oak tree! Wireless computer network and utilities included. Non-smokers. Deck, fireplace, wooded yard. $ _____ & $ _____ for larger room per month, includes utilities. Call (Your first name) at 727 / 000- 0000 or e-mail me at _____.

Clarkstown - Room Available. Call Shirley at 727 / 000 - 0000

Clarkstown - Room Available. Call Shirley at 727 / 000 - 0000

Clarkstown - Room Available. Call Shirley at 727 / 000 - 0000

Clarkstown - Room Available. Call Shirley at 727 / 000 - 0000

Clarkstown - Room Available. Call Shirley at 727 / 000 – 0000

APPENDIX ... LOTS OF HELPFUL QUESTIONNAIRES AND OTHER ITEMS FOR YOU! ▪ 205

Room for Rent – Phone Interview Questionnaire

Name: _____ Phone #: _____/_____ Date: _____

Where are you presently living? _____

Where are you currently working? _____

Type of Job: _____

Would this location be good for you? _____

How long have you been in this area? _____

Any family in the area? _____

Where do you go to church? _____ How long? _____

When did you come to know the Lord? _____

Furniture? _____ Size of bed? _____ Storage? _____

Morning or late night person? _____ Allergies? _____ Animals? _____

Do you like a room that is cooler or toasty warm? _____
My rooms are on the lower level and is cooler than upstairs.

Would you say that you are generally messy or tidy? _____
You would be responsible to keep your living area somewhat tidy and clean your bathroom.

Do you like to cook or do you tend to eat on the run? _____ There would be cupboard space for you in the kitchen. Refrigerator downstairs. You are welcome to use the kitchen and feel at home, but of course, any items you use must be washed and the kitchen left tidy and ready for the next person. There should never be a time when dishes are left in the kitchen sink.

How long have you been looking? _____ When do you need to move? _____

What is it that you like about our home that is different from what you have seen?
_____

Of all the ads in the paper, why would you call an ad for a Christian family?_____
_____

Rent includes utilities (water, electric, heat, air conditioning), FIOS wireless Internet, TV, kitchen and laundry privileges, use of deck, fireplace, wooded yard.

Rent: $ _____ Is that similar to what you are paying now? _____

Security Deposit: $ _____. Will that be a hardship for you? _____

Rent is due on the 1ˢᵗ of the month and I make it a policy not to have to ask for it, but would expect you to be responsible and mature to provide it on or before the day it is due.

APPENDIX ... LOTS OF HELPFUL QUESTIONNAIRES AND OTHER ITEMS FOR YOU! • 207

Housing Agreement

125 Pleasant Way, Anywhere, State 30000

Our prayer is that our time together will be a blessing to you and that we might mutually grow in our walk with the Lord. We desire our home to be a place where we can rest from the pressures of the workplace and grow together as we develop a friendship.

Name: _____ *Arrival Date:* _____

Employer: _____ *Work Phone #:* _____

Cell Phone #: _____ *E-Mail:* _____

Birthday: _____ *Allergies:* _____
  Month / Day / Year

Vehicle – Make & Model: _____ *Color:* _____
License #: _____

* _____ Copy of 2 Recent Pay Stubs * _____ Driver's License * _____ References

In Case of Emergency, contact info:

Name: _____ *Phone #:* _____

Address: _____

Monthly Rent: $ _____ **Due on the 1<u>st</u> of each month** which includes room, use of kitchen & laundry, utilities (water, electric, heating and air conditioning), FIOS Wireless Internet and TV. **As a matter of principle and maturity, I do not expect to need to ask you for your monthly rent payment.** If I am not home, just place it in an envelope with my name on it at my place at the kitchen table on or before the 1st of each month. Thank you.

Security Deposit: $ _____ to be held as last month's rent   Paid On: _____

Please provide one month's notice when you plan to depart. Departure Date: _____
The door swings both ways, and I can request that you depart with a month's notice.

We are glad that you are here and pray that this will be a mutually rewarding experience for all of us. Please let me know right away if something is broken or not working properly in the house so that I can attend to it immediately for you.

We try to keep our home reasonably neat and clean and would expect the same in your living area. There is a vacuum in the laundry area, which is available for your use. The kitchen is fully stocked with utensils, etc. and a cupboard will be provided for some of your food items. A refrigerator in the laundry area is provided for your use.

Our rule in the kitchen is if you use it, wash it and clean up after yourself. There should never be a time when dirty dishes are left in the sink. As a matter of principle, all guests will be entertained in the common use areas of the house and yard. Trash pick up is Tuesday and Friday early AM so trash should be put out the night before at the bottom of the driveway (away from the mailbox).

Signature: _____   Date: _____

Housing Etiquette ... It takes "team effort" to make a house feel like a home!

Ladies,

As we share this home together, know that it will take "Team Effort" to help keep our home fresh, clean, and enjoyable for all ... and ready for guests when they stop by!

✓ **Kitchen Reminders ... "Kitchen Etiquette"**

- ❖ If you use it, please get in the habit of washing your dishes as you prepare your food, so it is easy clean up when you are done and so that the next person comes to a clean sink! ☺

- ❖ If you spill something ... take a moment and clean it up. Don't just leave it for the next person ... whether it is a spill in the "Refrigerator," into "the Stove," or "on the Kitchen Floor" ... we do have a broom, a dust pan and a mop that work well. Rinsing the sponge keeps it "Fresh!"

- ❖ Please off load the drainer if it is full ... "before" you add more dishes to it and it overflows!

- ❖ Please "Do Not" use forks and knives in the frying pans ... as they will scratch the surface! Please take the item out of the pan and put on a plate to cut!

- ❖ Please wipe off the stove of crumbs, spices, or spills ... and clean the burner if your pot overflows.

- ❖ Please, use the broom and dust pan to clean up spills and to help keep the kitchen floor clean.

- ❖ Plastic, glass, cans and cardboard cereal boxes, etc. are recyclable ... Please do not leave on the kitchen counter. There are plastic bags below the kitchen sink to gather them to take out to the garage.

- ❖ We all contribute to the kitchen trash. When you see that it is full, please take a little initiative to tie it up, put it by the front door and replace the bag with a fresh one. The next person out the front door can help get it to the garbage cans … even if it is you!

- ❖ Trash is picked up very early on Tuesday and Friday. If you notice it needs to go out, please help get the trash cans to the bottom of the driveway … or bring up the empty cans.

- ❖ No kitchen glasses, coffee mugs or silverware are to leave the house. Please use plastic silverware or Styrofoam cups for items you are taking to your car.

- ✓ *<u>Vacuum Etiquette</u>* … We do have a vacuum and it just needs to be plugged in and pushed to work! Please take the initiative to help keep our home presentable. If something spills, please be quick to clean it up.

- ✓ *<u>Bathroom Etiquette</u>* … Please keep your bathroom tidy and clean so mildew doesn't grow and it is fresh when guests come to visit. Every week or every other week a little cleanser or cleaner does wonders to give your bathroom the "Fresh Smell & Look."

- ✓ *<u>Laundry Room</u>* … It is important to remember that your clothes will dry a whole lot faster if you get in the habit of emptying the filter in the dryer before you turn it on. It also saves on electricity!

- ✓ *<u>French Door</u>* … Please remember to "open" the screen and slide it back before closing the French Door. It will close much easier that way. Thanks!

- ✓ *<u>Items that 'Don't Work or "Get Broken"</u>* …Please, please let me know if anything "doesn't work" or "gets broken" … so we can get it repaired, whether it's a window curtain that doesn't stay up, caulking that is coming off around the tub, a leak, whatever! I would rather know so that it can be addressed before it becomes a major problem!

✓ *TV* ... We all know there is a ton of trash on the TV and it is easy to get sucked into watching a show. Please guard your heart and mind and watch only those shows that would honor the Lord and those who live in this home. I have prayed throughout our home that Satan would not take a foothold in any room or any life and need your help to keep the standard high and above reproach! Philippians 4:8

Items to Remember as you are Planning to Move on to the Next Chapter of Your Life...

When you are planning to move on to the next chapter of your life, please remember to clean up and make sure things are ready for the next person ...

- ✓ Clean out your refrigerator and clean up spills

- ✓ Clean your bathroom so it is Fresh and sanitized

- ✓ Vacuum your room

- ✓ You may want to buy a roll of packing tape for use with your boxes

- ✓ Remember to forward your mail to your new home address

- ✓ Please leave the house key on the kitchen table

- ✓ If you use any of my tarps to keep your items dry on a rainy day, please return them promptly so they are available for the next person.

Eviction Notice ... I hope you never need to use this one!

Date: _____

Keith & Dianne,

Thank you for meeting with me on Tuesday evening, March 9th, 2010 to discuss issues that have developed over the past week and a half.

As per our House Meeting this evening, and in line with the rules of your signed Housing Agreement, consider this letter your 30 day written notice to vacate the premises. You are expected to have completed moving your belongings and to have vacated the premises located at 125 Anywhere St, Somewhere, VA 37192 by 5:00 PM, Friday, April 9th, 2010.

As I stated in our meeting, if you have your things out of the house and garage prior to Saturday, March 27th, 2010 and have completed the checkout list provided, I will refund any balance for the month of March to help you with your financial situation. If you are here through April 9th, 2010 your prorated amount for these 9 days will be $ _____ which will be due on April 1st, 2010.

If you need assistance in acquiring housing you may wish to call Coordinated Services Planning of Fairfax County at 703 / 222-0880 for housing and resources. By calling this number you may be provided other resources including up to 18 months of subsidized rental assistance.

Sincerely,

Shirley Kimball

I have received this 30 day notice to vacate.

_____   _____   _____   _____
Keith (Last Name)   Date   Dianne (Last Name)   Date

Questions to Ask "Before You Marry!"

❖ *<u>General Balance</u>*

1. Do you feel intellectually equal to your partner?

2. Do you feel socially equal to your partner?

3. Do you have an interest in learning?

4. Is there inequality in education that could cause a problem?

5. Do you find it easy to mix with other people?

6. Are you ill at ease in a group?

7. Do you tend to tire more easily than the other?

8. Are you generally particular about dress and neatness?

9. Is style important to you?

10. Are you in favor of racial integration?

11. Are you interested in getting involved in community affairs?

12. Do you tend to keep well informed?

13. Do you have an interest in your neighbors? Have you taken the time to get to know any of them?

14. Do you like to read?

15. Do you like to discuss and share ideas?

16. Do you enjoy humor? Jokes? And Stories?

17. Do you ever have trouble getting your ideas across to the other?

18. Do you agree on politics – party, international affairs, war, etc?

19. Is there much difference in family background? (wealth, customs, etc.)

20. Do you consider your partner to be a strong or weak personality?

21. Are you able to get along without modern luxuries if necessary?

❖ *Communication*

1. Are there any witticisms or manners of speech in the other that annoy you?

2. Is there anything about the voice of the other that annoys you?

3. Is there anything about the silence of the other that annoys you?

4. Can you be absolutely honest with each other without fear?

5. Are you able to keep cool in an argument?

6. Do you find that discussion with you often turns into an argument?

7. Do you tend to neglect taking care of little problems daily and let them accumulate?

8. Do you meet suggestions for change without bristling or temper?

9. When you have differences, do you tend to go immediately and get them resolved?

10. Have you been called stupid or bull-headed?

11. Can you be at ease with each other for long periods of time without saying a word?

12. Do you ever feel that you know what the other is thinking before it is said?

❖ *Your Tastes and Preferences*

1. Do you find agreement in taste when you window shop?

2. Do you agree on furniture?

3. Do you like plain things?

4. Do you settle for things that look alright but which may be cheap?

5. Are you fussy in buying?

❖ *Money*

1. Are you against the wife working?

2. Are you in agreement that you should save, and the percentage of your income to be saved?

3. Are you against the wife having a say in setting the budget?

4. Are you against the wife controlling the check book?

5. Are you in agreement about giving to the Lord?

6. Do you agree on insurance or other forms of building an estate?

7. Are you in agreement on saving for your children's education?

8. Do you want a joint checking account?

9. Do you approve of borrowing money?

10. Do you approve of borrowing from your families?

11. Are you generally thrifty?

12. Do you tend to favor economy over quality?

13. Are you willing to seek the advice of an estate planner?

❖ *Health*

1. Do you like plain food over spicy foods?

2. Do you exercise regularly?

3. Do you believe in regular health check-ups?

4. Do you tend to worry and be anxious?

5. Do you like fresh air in your bedroom at night?

6. Do you like your home on the warm side generally?

7. Do you generally maintain a regular eating schedule?

8. Do the schedules of your families coincide?

9. Do you require a lot of sleep to be at your best?

10. Do you rise early in the morning full of zest?

11. Do you have any physical defects that your partner should know about?

12. Is there a family health problem that your partner should know about?

13. Are you against mixed dating? Dating people of a different race or ethnicity?

14. Are you a slow person?

15. Are you prone to headaches, colds, stomach upset?

16. Do you have allergy problems?

17. Have you read anything on human physiology?

18. Do you think that sex for pleasure between husband and wife is sinful?

❖ *Children*

1. Are you in agreement on the number of children you want?

2. Do you agree on the form and method of discipline to use?

3. Do you plan to space your children?

4. Are you informed on how to do this?

5. Are you in agreement to have children?

6. Have you talked about what method of contraception you will use?

7. Are you willing to adopt in the event you are unable to have children?

8. Are you agreed on the purpose for having and raising children?

9. Do you plan to bring them up the way you were brought up?

❖ *Family Policies*

1. Do you plan to visit each other's families occasionally?

2. Are your families the kind that will meddle?

3. Do you approve of separate vacations?

4. Do you agree on who should get birthday and anniversary gifts in your extended family?

5. Do you like to entertain in your home?

6. Do you think a husband and wife should have occasional time away from the children?

7. Do you want to have a pet in the house?

8. Are you agreeable to have an in-law (widow, etc.) living with you?

9. Have you discussed what to do if and when you have family discord?

10. Do you have personal devotions?

11. Do you want to have devotions together?

12. Do you wish to have them in the morning?

13. Do you wish to have them in the evening?

❖ *Recreation and Leisure*

1. Do you enjoy the same kinds of vacations?

2. Do you have the same travel interests?

3. Do you like the mountains?

4. Do you like the beaches?

5. Do you have hobby interests that you share?

6. Do you like the same kind of music?

7. Do you have a hobby that might be unfair to your partner in terms of time and money?

8. Do you watch television much?

9. Do you enjoy attending sports events?

10. Do you enjoy window shopping?

11. Do you enjoy gardening?

12. Do you enjoy painting?

13. Do you enjoy the same kind of reading?

14. Do you enjoy just being lazy?

15. Do you enjoy visiting museums?

16. Do you enjoy giving time to youth activities?

❖ *Aesthetic Values*

1. Do you have a cultural interest or a form of art that would irritate the other?

2. Do you find that you are compatible in appreciation of certain soaps, food odors, deodorants, colognes?

3. Are you a devotee of neatness?

4. Does disorder drive you to distraction?

5. Does an unmade bed disturb you?

6. Do unwashed dishes, etc. disturb you?

7. Do towels carelessly hung bother you?

8. Does a picture hanging crooked bother you?

9. Do dirty clothes left around bother you?

10. Was your mother meticulous in her housekeeping?

11. Are you annoyed if the other sings off key?

12. Would you like to see the other dress differently?

13. Do you become enraptured at a beautiful sunset?

14. Are you very color conscious?

❖ *Ethics*

1. Does it disturb you not to be able to pay a bill on time?

2. Do you become disturbed when your partner becomes involved with the opposite sex?

3. Do you become upset when you don't win a game?

4. Do you tend to exaggerate the truth?

5. Does your partner tend to keep his promise?

6. Does your partner seem at all to be self-centered?

7. Do the following bother you when done by someone else? <u>Underline behaviors that bother you:</u>

Picking teeth	Smacking lips	Blowing nose
Sneezing	Spitting	Manner of chewing
Scratching	Loud eating and drinking sounds	Twisting

Clearing throat	Snoring	Sniffing
Chewing gum	Personal grooming	Use of perfume
Use of cosmetics	Lateness (chronic)	Disorderliness
Leaving doors open	Leaving lights on	Leaving bathroom a mess
Kidding	Meticulousness	Ramrod formality
Excessive piety	Forgetfulness	Often loosing things

8. Can you forgive those who are repentant of gross evil?

❖ *<u>Sex</u>*

1. Can you talk about sex with open honesty?

2. Do you have factual understanding of male and female anatomy and function?

3. Do you believe that sex is evil?

4. Do you believe that it is sinful for married partners to see each other's nakedness?

5. Do you feel that your children should see their parents in various stages of undress?

6. Do you feel that if two people love each other it is somehow okay to have sex before marriage?

7. What does God's word say on this topic?

8. Do you believe strongly that you want to save the gift of giving yourself to your spouse as a wedding present?

Personal Characteristics

1. Have you ever seen your partner under stress or provocation?

2. Did you notice any strong emotional responses?

3. Are you or your partner moody?

4. Does this disturb you?

5. Have you ever been told that you are irritating?

6. Do you feel that you could understand and respond in love to your partner when they have made a mistake or accidentally broken something you value?

7. Do you think you could ever forgive your partner if they cheated on you?

8. Would you attempt to bring them out of this?

9. <u>Underline the traits you see in your partner:</u>

    Dreamy, indecisive, aggressive, submissive, domineering, morose, sedate, serious, active, happy, impulsive, flighty, bubbly, poised, slow, quiet, humble, appreciative, radiant, hateful, cruel, critical, crabby, fearful, conservative, realistic, adventuresome, idealistic, violent, forceful, convincing, repulsive, deceptive, suave, kind, loving, considerate, truthful, compassionate, generous, thoughtful, careful, meek, pleasant, willy-nilly, stingy, jesting, joking, belittling, humorous, fun-loving, sparkling, blustery, reliable, vivacious, drab, uncouth, profane, sensitive, thrifty, easily offended, reverent, irreligious, lazy, wasteful, positive, careless, sloppy, neat, orderly, punctual, clean, polite, stiff, easy-going, energetic, industrious, nervous, kittenish, calm, slap-happy, studious, logical, friendly, withdrawn, flashy, depressed, glum, confident, unclean, honest, optimistic, trustworthy, inspiring, unreliable, imprudent, wise, inquisitive, snoopy, intelligent, fastidious, insulting, selfish, prejudiced, tolerant, understanding, approachable, untruthful, enthusiastic, courteous, refined, gentle, tender, spiritual, rough, hard, stern, fair.

10. Now go back over the list and circle the traits that describe you. Have your partner do the same and compare your lists.

❖ *<u>Understanding</u>*

1. Have you had much association with the other sex in growing up?

2. When you see a flaw in another person do you tend to criticize? Ignore? Help?
(Underline your choice)

3. Are there questions which you do not feel that you can discuss with your partner?

Medical Coverage – Choices available other than COBRA

If you need medical coverage and want to keep the cost down, you may want to consider the samples below and then call the numbers listed and check out their websites to get more information so that you can make an informed decision based on your health needs. Plans change over time, but these will get you started on your way to finding less expensive discount plan coverage. I have National Better Living Association coverage and have been very pleased. My son, Josh, is college age and has coverage with United Health One. Understanding medical insurance can be very confusing, so I have created a spreadsheet so that you can match apples to apples to determine if one of these plans or another would be best for you.

Medical Insurance Categories	Global Med Benefits - GMB 800 / 979-4870	National Better Living Association 866 / 330-8332 x 105 Customer Service: 888 / 774-0848	United Health One 877 / 270-4713
Spoke with …	Christine	Ernest / Phyllis / Barbara	Ryan Sheridan
Insurance Co	US Life / Direct Med / Aetna CASA www.global-mb.com	US Life Insurance Co. 5 Underwriters of Ins. www.mynbla.com/hlsi/	United Health One
Cost:	**Select Plan** Member for Life PPO Network POS - Point of Service Medical Savings Assoc. Plan Enrollment: $135 One Time Fee Thereafter: $179 Per Month ……… Rate Never Goes Up! (Corporate Rate)	**NBLA 300 Premier** Member for Life PPO Network 1000 - Beechstreet Limited Benefits Plan Not a Health Discount Plan Enrollment: $100 One Time Fee Thereafter: $189 Per Month ……… Rate Never Goes Up! (Corporate Rate)	$86.35 per Month + $13.50 Mo. Dental/ Vision = $99.85 Month Apply on-line - Subject to Approval 2 Year Price Guarantee They pay 100% after deductible is met.

Medical Insurance	Global Med Benefits - GMB	National Better Living Association	United Health One
			$83.00 + $3.35 Administrative Fee = $86.35
	* No Medical Exam Required	* No Medical Exam Required	* No Medical Exam Required
Deductible $	* No Deductible	* You can change coverage up or down at any time - due to hospital stay or dental work needed, etc. * No Deductible	$2,500 - Max out of Pocket
PPO Doctor Network		With Pre-Negotiated Fees Beech Street PPO Doctor Network PPO Network 1000	Visit Any Doctor in any State
Doctor Visits	5 per year ... then negotiate price Unlimited visits - Negotiated price They pay $50 towards your 5 Dr. visits and negotiate rest of price. You end up paying $20 for the visit.	* 3 Accident/Sick visits per year ... Plan negotiates price. 30% off your bill for Network doctors. File claim for $50 reimbursement. * All other visits, check-ups and wellness visits paid at 30% discount. Unlimited visits - Negotiated price They pay $50 towards your 3 Accident/Sick Dr. visits and negotiate rest of price. You end up paying $20 for the visit.	Visit Doctor and they will send in paperwork and bill you contract rate - approx. $40 depending on type of Dr. They pay the rest until you meet deductible.
Diagnostic Lab Tests, CT Scans	Mammo, MRI, Pap, X-Rays, EKG covered @ 70% 70%	Mammo covered @ 50%, Pap, X-Rays, EKG covered @ 70% 70%	They have contract rate and bill you

APPENDIX ... LOTS OF HELPFUL QUESTIONNAIRES AND OTHER ITEMS FOR YOU!

Medical Insurance	Global Med Benefits - GMB	National Better Living Association	United Health One
Pharmacy ... Prescription Plan	4 Tier Generic $10 or Less (Walmart $4) Name Brand $20 or Less Top Brand $40 or Less Non-Formulary - Heavy Drugs for Cancer, Heart, Aids	If you choose Name Brand there is a $50 Annual Deductible Generic $12 - $24 or (Walmart $4) Up to 60% off on Name Brand Contact SAVRY 800/228-3108 for prescription questions. 3 month supply of prescription mailed	Preferred Price Card - Lowest Cost for the prescription at Pharmacy
Emergency Room	$100 Fee - That's All. Then plan covers up to $5,000. Then Major Med kicks in at 100%. Then covered 100%	$100 Fee - That's All. Then your benefits kick in at 73% Negotiated Rate. Then Plan Pays $50 Emergency Room Visit	All costs applied toward your deductible, then they pay at 100%
Hospitalization	Covered up to 70% of Bill Plan pays you $50 per day for 180 days - Indemnity Plan	Negotiation Service Plan Pays 73% Negotiated Rate, then pays you $300 day for a Hospital Stay	All costs applied toward your deductible, then they pay at 100%
ICU	Plan pays 70% - No $ per day - Can upgrade plan and receive $ for days in ICU	Plan Pays 73% Neg. Rate, then plan pays you $600 day for ICU to pay towards your negotiate rate bill.	All costs applied toward your deductible, then they pay at 100%
Accident Medical Benefit	Plan pays $500 Monthly Total Disability Benefit for 12 months	Accident Medical Disability Benefit paid up to $1,000	

Medical Insurance	Global Med Benefits - GMB	National Better Living Association	United Health One
Chiropractor / Alternative Med	30% Coverage		After deductible is met, they pay up to $2,000 benefit per year. Then future expenses are out of pocket.
Accidental Death / Dismemberment	$25,000 Coverage	Plan Pays Up to $5,000	
Dental	Aetna - 50% Across the Board	No Dental on this plan - Can upgrade to include Dental & Vision	$13.50 Mo + $15 Sign-Up Fee
Vision	Direct Med - 45% Across the Board Laser Surgery - 15% covered	No Vision on this plan	
Students	Says he can be covered to age 23, then apply for Individual Plan. Individual Plan would be $124 which includes Dr. visits at negotiated rate and $10,000 Accidental Death / Dismemberment for this price. Family Plan would be $299 At age 23 student can get his own plan for $179 with same coverage as above.	Says he can be covered to 24 whether a student or not. As part of the Family plan, *add $110* for total of $299. Individual Plan would be $189 Family Plan would be $299	

CD's and Annuities

Things to know about investing in a CD (Certificate of Deposit) or Annuity to help save and produce during your retirement years! Remember ... Don't loose your principal cash ... Do grow your investment and get the bonus!

- ❖ CD (Certificate of Deposit) .... A simple way to invest and never loose your principal!

  - If you have some cash that you would like to see grow by gaining interest and you don't need it for 3, 6, 9 months or a year, then consider investing it in a CD. The positive is that you can never loose your principal (the initial amount you invest). That's a good thing and very different from investing in stock where it can go up or down. Make sure the bank you invest with is FDIC insured.

  - Go to *www.bankrate.com* to determine which bank has the highest interest rate across the country and the best rating.

- ❖ *Annuities* ... Do you ever receive those letters in the mail inviting you to dinner and a seminar regarding financial information? Well, I do, and a couple of years ago I decided to learn what products were out there and what ones might work best for me. A free dinner and getting to meet some new people was also a plus!

  Over time, what I learned is that there are a couple of different schools of thought and each believes their products are the best ... because that is what they are licensed to sell to you, the consumer! However, if you are wise, you will soon learn that some products have a lot of built in fees and a chunk of your principal can be lost, though you may never see it disappear in fees.

  Also, there is a huge difference in how your investment will grow depending if you are in a fixed, indexed or variable annuity. There is also a *fixed indexed annuity*, and after studying the options, this is the one I chose for myself because it gives me the flexibility each year on the anniversary date of my annuity to "choose" whether I want to go with a "fixed" percentage (if the market is down) for that year, or I can choose to be in an "indexed" annuity for that year (money invested in the S&P index ... when the market appears to be more stable and growing). ***And, depending on the product you choose, you may receive a 10% bonus on your total contribution! Now that's a GREAT Idea!***

Here are some key points that I have learned and would share with you to get you started on things to look for if you want to make sure you "don't loose your principal" and have steady growth in a highly volatile market!

- ❖ *Fixed Indexed Annuity:* "Investment Features of those I looked at are as follows:"

  - ✓ Fixed Annuities have the guarantee of "No Loss of Your Principal" ... And, they have the safety and security of CD's. I decided "not to participate in the downside of the market!"

  - ✓ Elimination of Market Risk. The market can NEVER cause you a LOSS. A "Fixed Indexed Annuity" is FREE from Market Risk.

  - ✓ Potential for Market Growth with base of at least 3% or 5% earnings if the market goes down. If it goes up you can earn 6%, 8%, 8.5%, 11.5% Cap

  - ✓ All Gains Locked in Each Year

  - ✓ Fixed Indexed Annuity gives you the choice each year of receiving a Fixed Amount of 3% or 5% (principal protected) ... Or Indexed (S&P 500, NASDAQ 100, etc. variable Rate ... Market based). Therefore, during the years I choose to be in Indexed Funds, my earnings will be tied to Market Index (S&P 500, NASDAQ 100, etc.) This means my account goes up when the market goes up. If it goes down, you are guaranteed 3%.

- ✓ Tax-Advantaged Earnings ... All Earnings are Tax-Sheltered Until Withdrawn. Interest is Tax Deferred 5, 7, 10, 14, 16 years ... depending on the product you purchase.

- ✓ Access to Money ... At age 59 ½ you are eligible for a liquidable percentage each year. You can take out 10% the 1st year, or 20% the 2nd year if you need it with No Penalty ... but obviously taking money out decreases your base amount. Charges and penalties apply for early withdrawal under age 59 ½. At age 70 you are required to take out a portion of your annuity.

- ✓ No Probate Fees or Delays. All Assets Bypass Probate at death as they are part of a Living Trust. Your Beneficiary gets the remainder that you have not taken out of your account.

- ✓ Reduces Social Security Tax as you will most likely be earning less 10 years from now if you are in your later years.

- ✓ No High Fees or Expenses ... ***You Keep Every Penny of Your Principal***.

- ✓ ***Bonus Indexed Annuity*** – Gives you 10% Bonus immediately on the $ you invest. Example: If you invest $100,000 you will receive an immediate $10,000 Bonus! You have up to one year to set up your initial investment. All the funds that are rolled into your annuity, whether from a CD, savings account, etc. are eligible for the 10% Bonus.

- ✓ ***Bonus Indexed Annuity with "Lifetime Income Benefit Rider"*** – Gives you 10% Bonus immediately and Goes Up to 8% Per Year GUARANTEED. There is a % fee for this type of investment. Example: Rider Guarantees Points – "Bifs" ... .004% cost to you = 40 Basis Points, therefore on $100,000 your cost is $450 a year (.45%) and you are GUARANTEED 8% compound interest.

- ✓ *<u>Fixed Indexed Annuity with Bonus & Rider</u>* – Example: Open your account with principal of $100,000 + $10,000 Bonus. After 10 years at 8% your account will be worth $210,000 Net.

<u>*The Fixed Indexed Annuity (FIA) represents an extremely RARE investment alternative that offers a unique blend of ALL of these elements*</u>.

- ✓ *<u>Fixed Indexed Annuity</u>* – <u>*Contract Features*</u>

  ➢ No Up-Front Fees

  ➢ Instant Cash Bonus (3% to 10%)

  ➢ No Annual Administration Fees

  ➢ No Asset Management Fees

  ➢ 10% Penalty – Free Withdrawals for 1st 10 Years

  ➢ 20% (or higher) Penalty-FREE Withdrawals for Nursing Home / Home Health Care. If you have a terminal illness or go into a nursing home, you can take your money out with No Penalty.

  ➢ 100% Penalty Free Withdrawals After 10 Years

- ✓ <u>*How Does your Financial Investor Make Money?*</u> With the type of Fixed Indexed Annuity I purchased, he is paid by the insurance company. My principal is safe.

- ✓ <u>*Insured*</u>: Not by FDIC as banks are … Insurance Companies are real assets. They are 85% liquid. They are required to have $100 in reserve for every $100 you invest with them.

✓ *Beware*: Variable Annuities are based wholly on the stock market (which can be like a roller coaster). You want to avoid those with 12B1 Broker Fees and/or Spread! Also, there are a variety of "Indexed Annuities" … so learn about how they differ. Variable Annuities have High Fees and your broker will make lots of your money and you will loose a lot of your principal.

Sample of items you will want to discuss and understand as you pursue what financial vehicle / product is best for you!

- After sitting in on a variety of financial dinners and meeting individually with a variety of financial planners, I chose to invest my money through **Rick Clark** and highly recommend him to you. He can be reached at ***Clark & Associates.*** *Phone: 703 / 796-0957.*

- Fixed Indexed Annuity (FIA) … American Equity Bonus Gold

- Example with investing $100,000

  - FIA with Bonus & Rider offers a 10% Bonus … If you contribute $100,000 you will receive a $10,000 Bonus
  - Base Interest … 3.25% Interest Base
  - Rider with Interest Cap … 8% Interest Cap
  - Rider … Income Account Benefit Rider – Guaranteed for Life
  - Required Minimum Distribution (RMD) – Take some out at age 70

Reflections

When it's all said and done, you won't see a U-Haul behind your hearse in your funeral procession!

Don't save it all for Christmas!!!

Remember to ... Live Well, Laugh Often, Love One Another!

- Live a life that is noteworthy in the place where you live. Leave a legacy for others to follow in your footsteps.

- Be available, usable, and pliable for God to mold you and make you after His will. You are like clay in the Potter's hands and He desires you to be His masterpiece. Will you jump off the table and run and fashion your own way, or will you let Him direct your steps and mold you for greatness and empower you for bringing others to know Him? It is a choice. Choose wisely for the stakes are high, the path is narrow but well lit, and the rewards are eternal.

- Your Dash: The line between the day you were born and the day you die ... Make it count!

- *As Dr. James Dobson said to his son, "When it's all said and done, be there." Be there in God's kingdom when your days on earth come to an end and I will be waiting to greet you on the other side.*

- *Lord Manifest Yourself in us.*

- *Pearls of wisdom ... What have you learned over the years you have lived? How can you positively influence another?*

- Till then, may He just bless you with the knowledge of His Presence.

- *May our Lord continue to drench you in His blessings!*

- *May He give you wings to fly and experience all He has for you!*

For this reason, I bow my knees before the Father, from whom every family in heaven and on earth derives its name, that He would grant you, according to the riches of His glory, to be strengthened with power through His Sprit in the inner man; so that Christ may dwell in our hearts through faith; and that you, being rooted and grounded in love, may be able to comprehend with all the saints what is the breadth and length and height and depth, and to know the love of Christ which surpasses knowledge, that you may be filled up to all the fullness of God.
Ephesians 3:14-19

REFLECTIONS • 237

About the Author ...

In a small town in Pennsylvania with one stop light, my dad built the home where I grew up. There were farms nearby, my grandparents lived less than a mile away and their property backed up to a dairy farm where I went on a field trip with one of my elementary school classes. I still remember seeing how they milked the cows and the bottles of milk being filled on a conveyor belt, labels being attached to the bottles making them ready to put on trucks to be delivered. Many years later, this little town now has a few more lights, town homes, single family homes and a shopping center!

During various years we had a dog, a stray cat that my Mom realized was expecting, so she put a box with soft bedding in my closet and when I came home from school one day, there were 5 baby kittens! Two were stripped tabby cats, one with a brown nose and one with a pink nose, one was all black with a little white under his chin, and one was a grey Persian kitten that we called "Mouse" who loved to lie in the sun … in the middle of the street! Not a wise choice!!! For a while we had fish. One Easter morning there were pretty colored chick-a-dees that we loved and nurtured and all the kids in the neighborhood came over to play with them, … and then they grew up. One day we came home from school and they were gone. Years later we learned that we did have chicken for dinner that night. Well, so go the chapters of life!

I have many fond memories of my growing up years. We played hop-scotch and double-dutch (it's a jump rope game for you young'ins) in the driveway with friends, marbles, ball and jacks, board games, roller skated in the basement (where I put my arm through a small pain of glass on the door trying to stop ... and still have a small scar near my right elbow to prove it! I made multicolored potholders and sold them to neighbors, and then sold greeting cards another year. We, my brother, sister and I, even decided we could make money selling lemonade on hot summer days, and then decided to beef it up a little and showed reel-to-reel kids movies in our basement. We charged 10 cents admission, sold popcorn and lemonade. We didn't know it at the time, but we were entrepreneurs!

Mom was always there for us and always made sure we had 3 solid meals a day. I can't thank her enough for instilling the value of eating a healthy breakfast, a good lunch and a solid dinner. Eating three solid meals helped us not to crave a ton of snacks and junk food and therefore to make wiser choices.

It was always fun on the occasions that she would make chocolate chip cookies, cakes and pies and we got to lick the bowl or the mixer beaters! Yum! I still like licking them today! What a fun memory that I have passed down to my son and others! Mom liked to sew and used to make doll clothes for my doll. I didn't realize it then, but now know that it was a labor of love! Have you ever looked at the size of a small doll's sleeves and pant legs ... just sewing and turning that tiny piece of material was a labor of love!!!

Mom was one of 11 children. My grandmom gave birth to all 11 at home and somehow lived to tell the story! She was quite an amazing women who lived to be 100 years old, had a great quick whit that would definitely catch you off guard, and knew how to stand up for herself with her 5 foot frame. We had many aunts and uncles who lived nearby, so during the holidays, our home was grand-central station, sometimes with 30 or more people filling the rooms! Year after year, on Christmas Eve, Mom would make 14 pies, Dad would put up the tree and put on the lights, and Mom would trim most of the rest of it, including the tinsel! I still don't know how she did it all on Christmas Eve! I have definitely "upgraded" that tradition. I discovered that Mrs. Smith makes awesome pies and I enjoy turning on my oven, "baking them" ... no muss no fuss ... and having the aroma fill our home! I do enjoy baking ... but not 14 pies!

Also, putting the tree up the week after Thanksgiving and leaving it up as long as possible (if it is a live tree) and until the cold weather subsides in early March if it is going back in the box is another change! I know that may sound drastic to some of you ... but like the song says, "Don't Save It All For Christmas Day!!!" Every cold wintry day seems like Christmas when it is snowing and you kick on the lights on the tree, turn on the music, light a fire in the fireplace and see the festive decorations throughout the cold days of winter! When the spring flowers begin to show their greenery, then I know it is time to pack it all up and transition to the glorious beauty of Spring!

My dad was truly a "Mr. Fix It" and he could pretty much fix anything and make it work. That doesn't mean it always looked the same, but it worked! I remember one time the base of a glass bud vase had broken and he wanted to put a wooden base on it. I assured him we could just throw it away ... but Dad grew up during the depression and then you just didn't throw anything away. He was definitely a "saver" of things, many, many things and those of us who knew him well, knew he would save napkins, among other things, from McDonalds and Senior Citizen meetings ... just because they were still good and he would tear them in half and save the rest ... just because he had learned not to be wasteful when money was tight. When I was married with my own home, I would put together a list of items I needed his help with when he came to visit. He would always bring along his drill, his saw, and his tool box. I was always amazed at how I had tried to "fix" something and couldn't get it right ... and yet Dad could have it "fixed" good as new in the blink of an eye. He built the home we grew up in and the cottage we enjoyed for many years. We even have our hand prints in one of the cement blocks coming up the walk-way to the front door of our summer cottage.

Mom & Dad were frugal and, as they say, things are often more caught than taught. If we didn't have the money, we didn't buy it. As I got older, I was even more amazed to learn that when they knew they would be in need of another car, they saved for it and bought it with cash. Paid in full. I can't say that I have been able to do the same, but I do save and put together a good down payment and make sure to pay the monthly loan amount, plus a chunk towards principle so I end up paying less interest and pay it off early. That's discipline … but ultimately I'm looking to be wise and able to start planning my next vacation that can be paid for with what would otherwise have been a ton of money spent on interest. I just saved by being frugal! I will be forever grateful that they instilled in me the philosophy that "if you don't have the money, you don't buy it" … now that's a novel thought!

It's good to create a "wish list" and add things to it that you think you "must have!" As you continue to save and add things to your list, you will be amazed that what you thought you couldn't live without last month doesn't make it in the top 10 a few months later!!! Thrift shops make me laugh all the way home, as I have found sooooooooooooo many wonderful dresses, suits, blouses, sweaters, skirts and slacks over the years that I am ready for a cruise, warm summer days, a ski trip or a black tie dance! Clothes, shoes and accessories are just fun and I love to mix and match with delightful results. So many people move, downsize or change décor that it was easy to pick up a nice rocking chair, dresser, etc. as well.

Dad played guitar by ear (couldn't read a stitch of music), and would sing and play for enjoyment. One day Dad brought home an accordion when we were kids and my brother took lessons. He wouldn't teach me … so when he wasn't home I followed the beginner book and taught myself how to play! Years later when we were in our late teens, early 20's, my brother, Johnny, bought an organ and learned to play with the gift of playing by ear and reading music. I followed suit and taught myself what I could figure out and then took lessons for about six months. With knowing how to read the right hand music, play cords with my left hand (like guitar music), and adding the side-man (drummer beats) and pedal, I could sit down and get lost in the world of music as I sang along. My sister, Sue, who is still 4 years younger (ha!), loves to sing and played clarinet. As I think about it now, she must have played by ear like my Dad, because I remember that she never seemed to practice and yet played in the high school band! My Mom loved to sing and she played the radio!

I learned years later that with all marriages, things were far from perfect in our home. Even with all the dysfunction (that I was totally unaware of while growing up), I felt loved, nurtured, and well cared for over the years. I am thankful that my grandparents as well as my parents gave me a heritage that is very different from the "throw away" society that has been part of my experience. Both my parents and grandparents were married more than 50 years. And though they weathered many, many storms which in today's society would have easily ripped them apart, they are a tribute to me of what it looks like to keep your vows and marry for better or worse, in sickness and in health, till death do us part.

Unless we go back and take seriously what God said and choose to understand what God meant when he said to leave father and mother and cleave to your wife ... we will continue to be a society that robs kids of growing up in a stable home with one father and one mother. Having a "healthy home" that provides warm fuzzies, nurturing, commitment, morals and values that are instilled in children almost seems to be a lost art! *We are so bombarded with Hollywood's drama and believe the lie that the "grass might be greener in our neighbor's yard" that we have lost the commitment to "run the race" and stay the course through thick and thin, i.e. Hebrews 12:1-3.*

The tragedy is that Satan laughs as today's kids often grow up without positive, nurturing role models, get shuffled from here to there, experience different rules at different homes and haven't a clue what a loving, nurturing family is supposed to look like. If we would only realize that there are many, many resources today to help us through the difficult times and go and get help. We knew trials would come. Choose not to throw in the towel when communication lines break down. *I highly recommend that you view the Love & Respect DVD series by Emerson Eggerichs. It will open your eyes and do wonders for your communication and your marriage if you follow these principles and learn to speak each other's mother tongue and love language!* Though you may have very different opinions on some things, if you see yourselves as "two good willed people," there is definitely hope for success in your marriage.

Take your marriage in for a "tune up" offered by Family Life Today at their Family Life Weekend Conferences. Even if you think there is no hope ... give them a chance to give you the tools for hope and restoration. There are many conferences to choose from in various locations all around the year! So consider getting away for a weekend that may be the ticket to open the lines of communication and give you a fresh start.

Choose to be the mature spouse and determine to be the first to go and get help, be accountable and get a re-alignment. From personal experience I know two married people can see things very differently when it comes to working through issues concerning attitudes, perspectives, not being willing to set boundaries, step-children, mother-in-law's, and truly hearing the heart of your spouse. When children from a previous marriage become part of the equation, it is extremely important that both parents be in agreement on issues and not let the child(ren) grow up like a weed. I firmly believe we would save many a marriage if we stopped letting our mind justify what some think their heart desires! This is a sign that tragedy is brewing and about to affect the lives of the whole family for years to come.

Time and time again life has proven that the grass is not always greener in your neighbor's yard, in another city, or another country! <u>Put your glasses on, talk to their friends and neighbors and you will see that there are weeds in their yard too!</u> Instead, why not cultivate the soil in your own yard! Learn your spouses love language. Get help to see things from their point of view ... which may be extremely different ... "not wrong but maybe very different" from your own filter. Pull out the weeds and plant new dreams today to rekindle the embers until they become a flame and keep the fire burning bright at home. You will be blessed for running the race and finishing well ... and your children will thank you!

Selfishness and pride are usually the two ingredients that keep us blinded and cause us to think the other person is our enemy! That is a lie!!! God can blend differences if you are willing to hear the heart of your spouse and do what it takes to make changes. You will reap the benefit when they truly feel loved and respected.

I have many, many fond memories of the years that I was married. I love to take pictures and have tons of photos that warm my heart, remind me of wonderful years, dreams fulfilled, travel, boating and fishing on warm summer days, our son in martial arts tournaments and on many soccer fields, family times and life as it unfolded. Jack was an Oceanographer and then a Senior Systems Engineer. I was an Executive Assistant working for Presidents & CEOs of Corporate America. I loved my husband dearly and though we faced trials and tribulations, as all marriages do, the word divorce was never an option for me. We sought out Christian counselors and a mediator. We went to Family Life Conferences and attended church regularly. We both were Christians and both taught Bible Studies before we were married. Jack attended Westminster Seminary the year after we were married, and his daughter, Wendy age 10, called and came to live with us that same year. We put her in Christian school and saw major benefits. She began to smile naturally and that was a sure sign of improved self-image, along with grades that were drastically improved. She was starting to blossom and the fruit of our labors and God's blessings were on her life.

With two tuitions, we lived on my salary and learned to add more water to the soup. One year we even gave each other cards for Christmas, and for our anniversary we had hot dogs by candlelight. Though money was very tight, we had much to celebrate. We had our health, our family that was blossoming, our faith in a God who provided in amazing ways, and hope for a better tomorrow. We celebrated us and were thankful that God brought us through storms, over mountaintops, through valleys and gave us glimpses of hope for a better tomorrow.

Ten years after we married, God answered our prayers and graciously blessed us with a son who truly has the best gifts of both of us. Josh's heart for people, his love for the Lord from the age of 3, a growing faith, his laughter and zest for life, and his desire to be all that God wants him to be, continues to bring us great joy. His accomplishments as a biology / pre-med major at Campbell University while traveling with his college soccer team, and taking on the role of President of Fellowship of Christian Athletes for 3 years showed his commitment to excellence and to ministry for the Lord. I truly treasure every moment that I have the pleasure of spending with him! What a treasure he continues to be again and again.

We all know that life has some chapters and circumstances that we would like to avoid, and I assure you that after 21 years of marriage, I could not have made it through the trauma of divorce without the loving care of my parents, and my sister & her husband, Sue & Ned, who were there for me in so many ways. Spending holidays in Connecticut with my sister's family helped to ease the devastating pain of lives ripped apart. Their many, many loving, nurturing, caring ways made holidays bearable. Loving arms, wonderful food, warm flickering fires in the fireplace, music, laughter, gifts, hugs, family ties, and much more some how fed the soul of a wounded soldier in this battle for survival in our world. I went through times of feeling paralyzed and unable to function.

For five years I experienced severe depression and often wondered if I would ever find the key to unlock the door to feel alive again. I felt misunderstood, unloved, abandoned, rejected and deserted like an old shoe tossed to the wind. The scary part was that I wasn't sure I would ever break free of the depression long enough to have the will to pick up the broken pieces and figure out how to start over and begin to live again. I could not believe that divorce had walked up my driveway! Marriage is a dance between two people. When one stops dancing and is mentally, emotionally, physically and spiritually elsewhere, it is the death of a marriage, unless something happens to help the wandering spouse turn and realize what he is throwing away. Marriage requires communication, counseling, seminars where you gather new tools for your tool box and change on both parts. Every marriage whether good or on the rocks can use a yearly "tune up" and accountability partners and mentors throughout the year. Why try to reinvent the wheel when others more seasoned than you have walked through the highs and lows and can show you where the land mines are before you step on them?

As my world was crashing down around me, I discovered a video/seminar series at my church entitled DivorceCare that helped me process all that was happening and walked me through the steps of grief and recovery. I slowly began to heal from the pain and disbelief of the effects of divorce. A counselor asked me why I was letting someone who had walked away from our marriage have so much control over me. He was gone and mentally I was allowing his actions to keep me in depression. I had to start afresh with a blank canvas, figure out who I was, what my goals were, what new things I wanted to add into my world and who I wanted to become on this new journey. I had to figure out what pieces I could salvage and determine to "paint my world" with new colors and hues as I began to allow myself to live and feel again. It was a long process.

I'm a lefty and ambidextrous (like my Dad), and tend to run creative (like my Mom & Dad). I'm an A or AA type personality and strangers are just friends I haven't met yet! A warm smile and gracious heart that reaches out to nurture people I know or have just met makes life an adventure. I'm "the middle child" so I don't feel it needs to be done "my way," but I do have a variety of ideas and appreciate when they are considered as part of the equation. My love for the Lord, the gifts and talents He has bestowed on me, and all His many blessings toward me, inspires me to use this wonderful opportunity to share with others in a hurting world.

My 3 years on Young Life staff while I was in my 20's, spending summers at their camps and ranches opened a whole new world to me and blessed my life tremendously! Teaching Ladies Bible Study for 7 years showed me that the teacher learns as much if not more than the students! I encourage you to let your life shine, use your gifts and talents for a worthy cause, leave a legacy that counts when you stand before a Holy God, and be the music that someone else hears, whether through words, an act of kindness, your voice or a tune your life plays out each day! This is not a dress rehearsal …you are center stage … and God, your family, friends and those you influence each day you breath are your audience.

I love the poem that says:

"Some people come into our lives & quickly go. Some stay for awhile & leave footprints on our hearts and we are never the same."

I hope you've had as much fun reading and being nurtured by this book as I had in living the contents of it and writing it!

Remember to "Dance in the Rain!"

You may contact me at: *win4him7@gmail.com*

248 ▪ NOW THAT'S A GREAT IDEA!